Sewflakes

PAPERCUT-APPLIQUÉ QUILTS

Kathy K. Wylie

C&T PUBLISHING

Text copyright © 2007 by Kathy K. Wylie

Artwork copyright © 2007 by C&T Publishing, Inc.

PUBLISHER: *Amy Marson*

CREATIVE DIRECTOR: *Gailen Runge*

ACQUISITIONS EDITOR: *Jan Grigsby*

EDITORS: *Susan Beck and Kesel Wilson*

TECHNICAL EDITORS: *Georgie Gerl and Carol Zentgraf*

COPYEDITOR: *Wordfirm Inc.*

PROOFREADER: *Christine Mann*

COVER DESIGNER: *Christina Jarumay*

BOOK DESIGNER: *Rose Sheifer-Wright*

PRODUCTION COORDINATOR: *Matt Allen*

ILLUSTRATOR: *Kirstie Pettersen*

PHOTOGRAPHY BY *Luke Mulks and Diane Pedersen* of C&T Publishing
  unless otherwise noted

PUBLISHED BY C&T Publishing, Inc., P.O. Box 1456, Lafayette, CA 94549

Wylie, Kathy K.,

  Sewflakes : papercut-appliqué quilts / Kathy K. Wylie.

    p. cm.

  Summary: "Kathy shows you how to use papercut appliqué to tell your stories. From an image to a snowflake, from a block to a quilt, your own unique designs will emerge. Included are five quilt patterns that you can make or use as inspiration"--Provided by publisher.

          Library of Congress Cataloging-in-Publication Data
  ISBN 978-1-57120-495-0 (paper trade : alk. paper)
  1. Patchwork--Patterns. 2. Patchwork quilts. 3. Appliqué. 4. Cut-out craft.
  5. Snowflakes in art. I. Title.
  TT835.W977 2007
  746.46'041--dc22
            2007038139
Printed in China

10 9 8 7 6 5 4 3 2 1

Dedication

To the Creator of each exquisite snowflake and the Author of life.

Acknowledgments

Quilting can be a very solitary activity. Sometimes I fear I could become a recluse, for I truly enjoy the quiet days I get to spend alone, working on a quilting project. Yet I am not alone. There are wonderful people in my life, and I must take this moment to express my appreciation for their love and support.

To my quilting community, which shares this passion to create with fabric and thread: I am so grateful to the members of my quilting group, The Quiltsmiths, and in particular to Kirsten Johnston, for their advice and encouragement. They are just a few of the kind and generous quilters at York Heritage Quilters Guild who never fail to motivate and inspire me. A special thank-you to Donna Edwards for getting me started as a quilting teacher, and to my students for teaching me just as much as I taught them. One class was particularly loyal, and I'd like to thank Gail Chipperfield, Sheila Bond, and the rest of "QP7" for their friendship and extraordinary faith in me.

To my community of faith, my other "family": I wish to thank Jon Thompson for directing me toward this path, Rose Lynn Alexander for preparing me for the journey, and my dear friend Janet Hill for walking beside me every step of the way. I thank my God every time I remember you.

To the experts who contributed their talents to this project: I am indebted to Elly Sienkiewicz and Janice Lee Baehr for allowing their beautiful artistry to appear in these pages. It has been a privilege to work with C&T Publishing on this project. I wish to thank each member of the team for the dedication and expertise that transformed my ideas into these pages.

To my family, who know me best: My parents, Barb and Andy Kolada, somehow raised me to believe that I could do whatever I set my mind to. I thank my Dad for representing fatherhood well, for setting a fine example, and for loving me. I am most grateful to my Mom for spending so much time with me, for always being available to listen, and for being my friend.

I am very proud of my two wonderful sons, Tom and Mark. They have honored me with their respect and I thank them for their patience and understanding during this process. I owe the greatest thanks, however, to my husband, Bob. He has always understood my need to sew and has quietly supported me in so many ways. Without him, none of this would have been possible.

Introduction

As artists who create with needle and thread, we try to communicate through our work. Perhaps it is a little more difficult within the context of the "traditional" quilt because, after all, it is the *other* genre that is known as the "art" quilt.

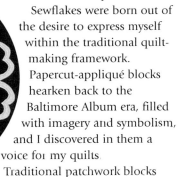

Sewflakes were born out of the desire to express myself within the traditional quilt-making framework. Papercut-appliqué blocks hearken back to the Baltimore Album era, filled with imagery and symbolism, and I discovered in them a voice for my quilts.

Traditional patchwork blocks also have an uncanny ability to speak, often just through their names. What does Double Wedding Ring or Lover's Knot or Contrary Wife say to you? The suggestion behind the name combined with the imagery of papercut appliqué makes a powerful statement. This is how I tell my stories.

Perhaps you don't think of yourself as an artist—yet. But you have stories to tell, too, even if your quilts don't hang in galleries and exhibit halls. The quilt you make for your grandson tells him that you understand his passion for basketball and that he is special to you. You express your love and your blessing in the wedding quilt you create for your daughter and son-in-law. Even the everyday quilts around your house have something to say about you.

This book shows you how to use papercut appliqué to tell your stories. From an image to a snowflake, from a block to a quilt, your own unique designs will emerge. Included are five quilt patterns that you can make or use as inspiration. I hope these pages will motivate and stimulate, and that you, too, will find a new way to communicate.

> *"Sewflakes were born out of the desire to express myself within the traditional quilt making framework."*

Contents

Let It Snow!

What Are Sewflakes?

Sewflakes are papercut-appliqué blocks. They are designed in the same manner as paper snowflakes, by folding paper and cutting a design. What makes sewflakes unique is the use of recognizable images as the foundation of the design. Sometimes the original motif is hidden once it is repeated and rotated within the sewflake, providing surprise and pleasure once the image is discovered.

Taken one step further, sewflakes can be combined with patchwork blocks to tell a story. Pieced blocks have such great names, which can be used to form a theme for the papercut-appliqué blocks. Think of the imagery suggested by blocks with names such as Log Cabin, Irish Chain, or Corn and Beans.

Surprise Designs

I can still remember the joy I experienced as a child making paper snowflakes. What a surprise to unfold that cut-up paper and discover such beauty within! I was so intrigued by the whole process that I made dozens and dozens of those lacy wonders, cut-ting each one differently so I could see the resulting effect. Decades later, I rediscovered the joy of that experience when I came across papercut appliqué.

I've always regarded Baltimore Album quilts with great interest and appreciation, and find myself particularly drawn to the papercut blocks. I love the geometry of them, their symmetry and simplicity. Usually stitched from a single piece of fabric, the papercut blocks provide a pleasing resting place for the eye among the colorful and complex wreaths, bouquets, and urns.

Hawaiian quilts, in contrast, showcase papercut creations, using them as the main event. Bold and beautiful, these blocks stand alone, often set in a single medallion against a heavily textured backdrop of echo quilting. How interesting it is to see the same technique used in such completely different ways.

At first glance, papercut-appliqué blocks seem to be just attractive appliqué patterns. There might be a flower bud, or a fleur-de-lis, or some leaves incorpo-

The Baltimore Beauties Album, 95˝ × 95˝, group quilt designed by and made under the direction of Elly Sienkiewicz, 1988-1993. Ruth Meyers appliquéd and embroidered the border, the center block, and set the quilt together. The sashing was made by Audrey Waite and quilted by Mona Cumberledge and Joyce Hill.

Photo by J. Mathieson

Midnight on the Oasis, 42˝ × 42˝, by Janice Lee Baehr. Pattern titled Orchid Oasis is available from Pacific Rim Quilt Company.

Photo by Janice Lee Baehr

rated into the design, but overall the block appears to be abstract. Closer inspection often reveals a different story. As I studied the papercut blocks in *The Best of Baltimore Beauties*, Books 1 and 2, by Elly Sienkiewicz (C&T Publishing, 2000 and 2002), I started to notice some hidden images. There was a cat in one block, and a violin in another—there was even an Eiffel Tower! I was intrigued by the possibilities.

I was curious to see how I could apply this technique to my quilts. The perfect opportunity arrived while I was designing *The Lord Is My Shepherd*, page 34, to depict the 23rd Psalm. One of the phrases from the 23rd Psalm reads, "Even though I walk through the valley of the shadow of death, I will fear no evil, for You are with me; Your rod and Your staff they comfort me." I folded a piece of paper, drew a shepherd's rod and staff along with a little lamb, and cut it out. The result was my first sewflake.

Rod and Staff block

Supplies

DESIGN SUPPLIES

• *Paper*—There are a few things to bear in mind when selecting paper for sewflakes. Multiple layers of thicker paper are harder to fold and cut than layers of thinner paper. You'll need paper the same size as your block size: for a 12″ × 12″ block, you'll need a 12″ × 12″ piece of paper. An economical option is to use flip chart or easel paper. These pads are roughly 2′ × 3′ in size and are readily available—just cut the pages down to the desired size.

• *Scissors*—Sharp scissors are essential. It is helpful to have a couple of sizes available: larger scissors for the rough cuts and smaller ones for fine, detailed cutting. Look for scissors with blades that come to a point at the end, as this will give you the greatest accuracy. I like the ergonomic design of the Fiskars Softouch scissors, which reduces hand fatigue.

• *Pencil and eraser*—I prefer to use a 0.5mm mechanical pencil so I don't have to worry about sharpening the lead.

• *Rulers*—I use an 18″ ruler for longer lines and a 6″ ruler for shorter ones. You should note that rotary cutting rulers are designed for use with a rotary cutter blade, not a pencil.

• *Protractor*—Because the paper will be folded into wedges, a protractor will help with measuring the angles at the base of the wedge. A small-size half-circle protractor, such as the one included in a classroom geometry set, is sufficient.

APPLIQUÉ SUPPLIES

The supplies required to appliqué sewflakes will vary depending on the type of appliqué you decide to stitch. For appliqué techniques, see Sewing Sewflakes, pages 19–21.

Basic Appliqué Supplies

• *Template material*—Based on the appliqué method you choose, you will need freezer paper, fusible web, or water-soluble stabilizer.

• *Marking supplies*—To transfer your design to fabric, a variety of marking supplies may be required, such as a mechanical pencil, a light-colored fabric pencil, or a fine tip fabric marker. The 18″ ruler will also be needed.

• *Scissors*—The same scissors that were used for designing your sewflakes may be used, unless you prefer to keep a separate set of scissors for fabric and paper.

Hand Appliqué Supplies

• *Appliqué needle*—I like to use a size 10 Sharp. Straw needles are a little longer and are also often used for hand appliqué.

• *Thread*—I recommend choosing a fine (50- or 60-weight) cotton or silk thread that closely matches the appliqué fabric in color.

Machine Appliqué Supplies

• *Presser foot*—For best results, use an appliqué foot on your sewing machine. A clear plastic foot offers excellent visibility.

• *Thread*—For the bobbin, use a cotton thread that matches the background fabric. For the needle thread, use 0.004mm invisible monofilament thread for hidden stitching, or machine embroidery thread for decorative stitching.

Folding Paper

In creating one-of-a-kind sewflakes, the design process begins by folding paper. It is at this stage that the size of the block and the number of times the image repeats within the block are determined.

Block Size

There is a direct correlation between the size of the piece of paper that is folded and the size of the resulting block. For example, if you fold a 12″ × 12″ piece of paper, you create a sewflake that fits in a 12″ × 12″ block. You may choose to appliqué the sewflake onto a larger square of fabric, leaving more room around the design, but you begin by folding a piece of paper the same size as your desired block size.

The folded paper yields a design space that is a fraction of the starting size, so a larger piece of paper will leave more room for a design than a smaller one will. For more detailed or intricate images, choose a larger block size.

Repetitions

The way the paper is folded determines the number of times the image repeats within the sewflake. If you fold the paper into fourths, the image repeats four times; if you fold it into eighths, the image repeats eight times. The most common frequencies of repetition are four, six, eight, and twelve.

The more times an image repeats, the smaller the design space. Fewer repetitions may be preferable for detailed or intricate images, whereas more repetitions will produce a more intricate-appearing design. All of this should factor into your choice of repetition frequency.

Consider the following examples. An image of a light bulb is a fairly simple image, whereas a maple leaf is more complex. Watch what happens when each image is repeated four versus twelve times, keeping the block size the same.

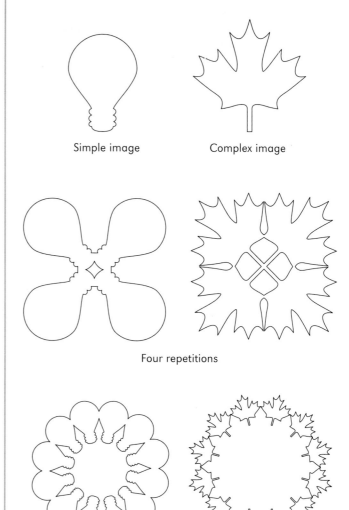

Simple image   Complex image

Four repetitions

Twelve repetitions

The simple image looks more interesting repeated twelve times, but the complex maple leaf is lovely repeated only four times. A much larger block size would be required to appliqué this sewflake of twelve maple leaves.

Folding

REPETITIONS	ANGLE
4	90°
6	60°
8	45°
12	30°

Wedge angles

To create a sewflake, the paper is folded into a wedge shape. The angle at the base of the wedge is equal to 360° divided by the number of repetitions.

FOLDING A 90° WEDGE—4 REPETITIONS

Option 1—Fold a square piece of paper in half diagonally, then in half diagonally again.

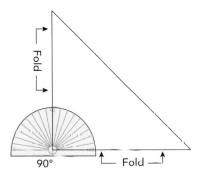

Folded 90° wedge – option 1

Option 2—Fold a square piece of paper in half horizontally, then in half vertically.

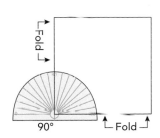

Folded 90° wedge – option 2

FOLDING A 45° WEDGE—8 REPETITIONS

1. Fold a square piece of paper in half diagonally, in half diagonally again, then in half a third time.

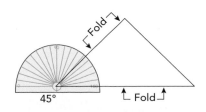

Folded 45° wedge

2. At this point, one side of the wedge is longer than the other side. Measure the short side and mark this measurement on the long side. (The short side measurement will be half the original page size. If the page size was 12″ × 12″, the short side measurement will be 6″.) Draw a line joining these points. Cut on the drawn line.

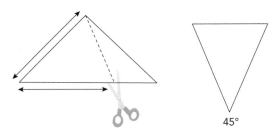

Measure and cut sides of 45° wedge.   Finished 45° wedge

FOLDING A 30° WEDGE—12 REPETITIONS

1. Fold a square piece of paper in half diagonally, in half diagonally again, then in thirds.

I recommend using a protractor for greater accuracy. Lay a protractor on the folded 90° wedge so that the base line is on one folded edge and the 90° line is on the other. Mark 30° and 60° on the paper.

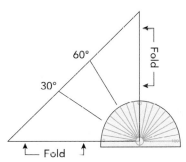

Mark 30° wedge with protractor.

2. Align one folded edge with the furthest marking and fold. Open the fold to reveal the crease, align the other edge with the crease line, and fold. Refold the first fold.

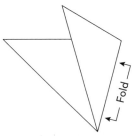

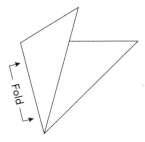

Align edge with furthest mark and fold.   Align opposite edge with crease line and fold.

3. Notice that the 30° wedge has "dog ears"; trim away excess paper as shown.

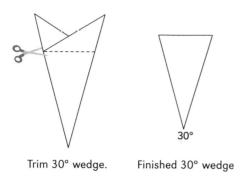

Trim 30° wedge. Finished 30° wedge

FOLDING A 60° WEDGE—6 REPETITIONS

1. Fold a square piece of paper in half diagonally, then in thirds.

To divide a 60° wedge into thirds using a protractor, measure the long folded edge with a ruler and divide this measurement by 2; this will be the midpoint. Mark the midpoint, and lay the protractor so that the base line is on the fold and the 90° line is on the midpoint. Mark 60° and 120° on the paper.

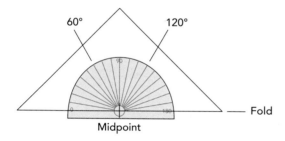

Mark 60° wedge with protractor.

2. Working from the midpoint, align one half of the folded edge with the furthest marking and fold. Open the fold to reveal the crease, align the other edge with the crease line, and fold.

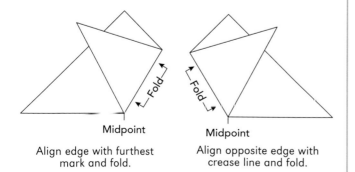

Align edge with furthest mark and fold.

Align opposite edge with crease line and fold.

3. Refold the first fold, and cut away the excess the paper.

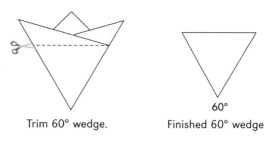

Trim 60° wedge. Finished 60° wedge

MARKING THE CENTER OF THE WEDGE

It is often useful to mark the centerline on the wedge before beginning a design. This is especially true for drawing symmetrical images. Once again, a protractor is the best tool for the job.

REPETITIONS	ANGLE	CENTER
4	90°	45°
6	60°	30°
8	45°	22.5°
12	30°	15°

Wedge centers

The center of the wedge is one half of the angle at the tip of the wedge. Lay the protractor on the folded wedge so that the base line of the protractor is on one folded edge and the wedge angle is on the other. Mark the center degree measurement on the paper. Using a ruler, draw a line through the mark to the tip of the wedge.

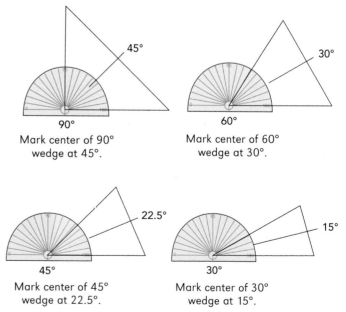

Mark center of 90° wedge at 45°.

Mark center of 60° wedge at 30°.

Mark center of 45° wedge at 22.5°.

Mark center of 30° wedge at 15°.

Designing Sewflakes

Designing sewflakes is a process that begins with folding paper and continues with drawing, cutting, and unfolding.

To illustrate the basic concepts of designing sewflakes, we will begin with a simple, symmetrical shape: a heart. Fold a 12″ × 12″ piece of paper according to the number of times you want the image to repeat—for example, 8 times (a 45° wedge) for 8 image repeats. Draw the image onto the folded wedge of paper and cut it out. Then, unfold the paper to discover the surprising design within!

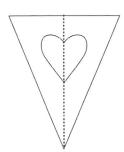

45° wedge creates sewflake with 8 hearts.

If the same heart is drawn onto a 12″ × 12″ sheet folded 12 times into a 30° wedge for 12 image repeats, this is the resulting sewflake design:

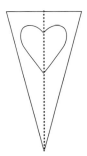

30° wedge creates sewflake with 12 hearts.

Now you may want to add some shape to the outer edges of the design to create a sewflake like this:

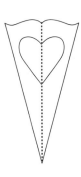

Trimming the outer edge creates scalloped-edge sewflake.

Cut away a portion of the center and the look changes yet again!

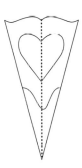

Trimming a large portion of inner edge creates sewflake with large center.

If the hole in the center is too large, make it smaller.

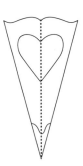

Trimming a small portion of inner edge creates sewflake with small center.

Tip To cut elements from within the folded paper wedge, you need to make a hole to insert your scissor blade into. If you find there are too many layers of paper to poke a hole with the tip of your scissors, try folding the paper at the location for the hole and taking a small cut through all the layers.

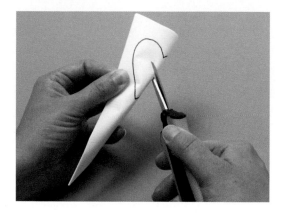

After you unfold the paper sewflake, you can assess your design and make whatever changes you feel are necessary. With a few more adjustments, the completed sewflake design might look like this:

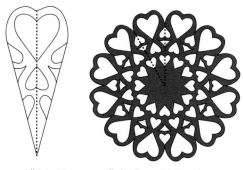

All My Heart sewflake from 30° wedge

Positive vs. Negative

The previous examples are all negative images, which means that the image appears in the background as a result of cutting away the foreground.

If you want to create a positive image, and have your motif appear in the foreground, cut away the background of the paper to leave only the image.

Continue working with the heart motif. Fold the 12″ × 12″ square of paper 8 times into a 45° wedge for 8 image repeats. *This time, draw the heart large*

enough to reach the folded edges of the 45° wedge. Part of the heart will remain within the fold, so when it is cut out and unfolded, 8 hearts will be joined together in a positive image.

My Valentine sewflake from 45° wedge

Tip There is no right side up or upside down in a sewflake; the image will be rotated in all directions. Work with the wedge shape to determine the best fit for your image. A heart is wider at the top, so it makes sense to place it at the widest point of the wedge.

Symmetrical Motifs

What is the difference between the two wedges shown below? The first shows the right half of a heart drawn on the left fold and the left half drawn on the right fold. The second has the heart centered on the wedge. The difference? None!

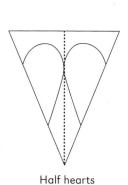

Half hearts   Half hearts sewflake

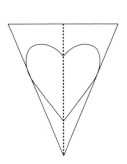
Centered heart

Centered hearts sewflake

A heart is a symmetrical shape, which means that the left half is identical to the right half. Whatever you draw on the fold will repeat in mirror image on the other side. Drawing half a heart on the fold produces a complete heart unfolded. To further illustrate this point, let's draw half a heart on one fold and half a flower on the other fold. The resulting design has four hearts alternating with four flowers.

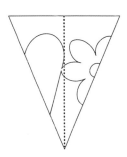
Half heart, half flower

Half heart, half flower sewflake

With symmetrical motifs, you have the option of drawing them on the fold or in the center of the wedge. *Nonsymmetrical images, however, must be drawn within the wedge.* A heart is only symmetrical vertically. Nonsymmetrical motifs will still alternate with their mirror image once the paper has been unfolded.

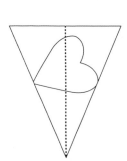
Sideways heart

Sideways heart sewflake

When working with positive images, symmetrical or not, it is important to remember that a portion of the motif must touch the fold on both sides. Otherwise, the sewflake ends up in pieces. Similarly, if there is more than one motif within the wedge, each element must touch another element so that it is connected with the rest of the design. Avoiding these common mistakes will ensure that you unfold happy surprises!

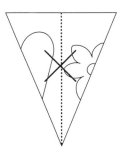
Heart not touching fold (creates 4 double hearts)

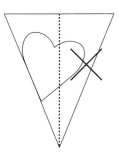
Half heart and half flower not touching (creates 4 hearts and 4 flowers, unjoined)

Heart and flower not touching (creates separate 8-flower sewflake and 8-heart sewflake)

Tip When drawing a symmetrical image within the wedge, here's a simple trick to help make

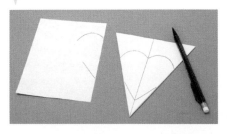

both halves of the image the same. Draw the first half onto the folded wedge. Take a scrap piece of paper and trace the half with a pencil. Turn the scrap paper over and line up the tracing with the original drawing. Trace again from the back of the scrap paper and the pencil will transfer the other half of the image onto the wedge.

Outer Designs

All the sewflake examples shown to this point have created inner designs to be appliquéd to the inside of a block. But these same papercut techniques can be used to produce extraordinary outer designs as well, designs that would frame the outside of a block.

To design this type of sewflake, work with a square sheet of paper folded into fourths or eighths *without trimming the long diagonal edge*, which keeps the square shape intact (see Folding a 90° Wedge and Folding a 45° Wedge, page 7). *Trace design elements along the non-folded edge.*

Wouldn't this make a lovely frame for a patchwork heart or a novelty print?

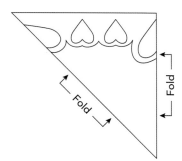

45° wedge with hearts and scallops

Open Hearted sewflake

Keeping the outer edge straight allows the perimeter of the design to be sewn right into the seam along with the rest of the block. But that doesn't mean you can't cut those edges. In this final example, small and large hearts are connected with a ribbon; both edges are cut away. This design would work well appliquéd over the seam between a block and its sashing, so that a different fabric would appear on each side.

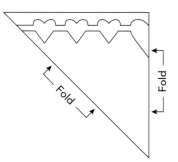

45° wedge with hearts and ribbon

Straight to the Heart sewflake

As you experiment, you will produce a collection of paper sewflakes. Keep the ones you like, and sign and date them. These papercuts are invaluable design aids, because they allow you to visualize how your design will look before you begin to work with fabric. They also serve as templates for creating accurate master wedges, as you will see in Preparing a Sewflake Pattern, pages 15–18.

Refining the Center

The center of a sewflake deserves special consideration, as the eye is inevitably drawn inward. The middle can be a focal point, making a bold statement about the block. It can also serve as a unifying element between multiple blocks. For these reasons, you may often find it useful to begin your design from the center and work outward.

The important thing to remember is that the middle of a sewflake will be magnified by the number of repetitions. *This means that even a small cut in the base of the wedge turns into a much larger hole when the paper snowflake is unfolded.* The way you cut the center can make or break your design.

Single Image in the Center

Using a single image in the middle turns the center of the sewflake into an important focal point.

For negative image designs, leave the base of the wedge uncut until the design is complete. Unfold the paper sewflake, then add one single motif in the middle, as in the quilt *King of Hearts*, page 58.

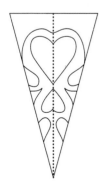 

All My Heart wedge   All My Heart sewflake

For positive image designs, consider appliquéing a single motif to fill a large interior space. For example, the sewflake Apple Pie would have a very large gap if used on its own in a block. A single apple, appliquéd in the center, fills the space and provides a focal point.

Single apple surrounded by Apple Pie sewflake

For a completely different look, fill the space with patchwork.

Apple Pie sewflake on Pineapple block

Consistent Centers

When designing multiple sewflakes for one quilt, keeping the centers the same will provide visual consistency. You can either begin by designing the center shape, or take the center shape from one sewflake and use it for all the others.

In the quilt *Tools of the Trade*, page 27, I really liked the star shape formed by the scissor blades in the Cut It Out sewflake, so for each subsequent block, I drew the same lines at the base of the wedge and worked the rest of the design around this motif.

Shepherd's Light block

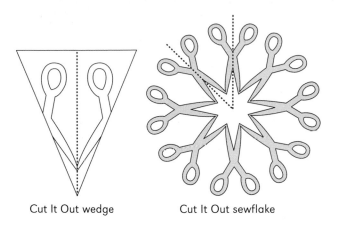

Cut It Out wedge   Cut It Out sewflake

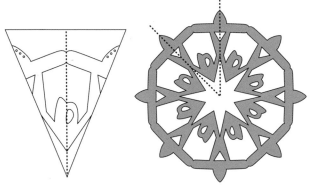

Pressing Matters wedge   Pressing Matters sewflake

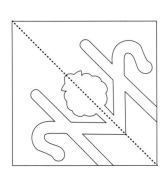 

Rod and Staff wedge   Rod and Staff sewflake

Pairing sewflake blocks with patchwork blocks can also provide the inspiration for the center shape. In the quilt *The Lord Is My Shepherd*, page 34, the patchwork block, Shepherd's Light, is essentially an eight-pointed star. I began each sewflake design by drawing that shape first at the base of the wedge.

Preparing a Sewflake Pattern

By now, I hope you've tried folding some paper and cutting a few sewflakes! If you have, you may have noticed that your paper sewflake is not completely accurate. This is because of the number of folds in the paper. Design elements that land on the fold will cut out slightly differently from the first inner fold to the last outer fold. Although the paper sewflake is a great design aid, it is not sufficiently precise to be used as a pattern for sewing.

As a result, we need to make a master wedge of our design. Time spent creating an accurate master wedge at this stage will be of great benefit when it comes time to transfer your design to fabric.

Making a Master Wedge— Symmetrical Designs

To create a blank master wedge, first determine the number of repetitions and the block size for your sewflake. On a piece of paper, use a ruler to draw a straight line that measures one-half of the block size. Use a protractor to mark the angle at the base of the wedge (see Folding Paper, pages 6–8). Draw another line the same length as the first on this angle. Connect the two ends to form the wedge shape. The full-size patterns provided in this book may also be used to trace a variety of master wedge sizes, or you can download blank master wedges from my website at www.kathykwylie.com.

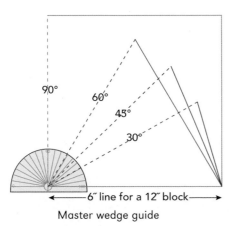

Master wedge guide

Choose the best wedge from the paper sewflake to trace. This is usually the wedge with your original drawing lines on it. Lay the paper sewflake on top of the blank master wedge, lining up the fold lines with the master wedge lines. Use a pencil to carefully trace around the cut out areas.

Trace sewflake to master wedge.

Remove the paper sewflake and assess. Are there any curves that need smoothing or lines that need straightening? Does the center of the design line up with the center of the wedge? This is the time to clean up your design and make it perfect.

For symmetrical designs, anything that touches the left side of the wedge must line up with the right side of the wedge. Measure from the tip of the wedge on each side and make adjustments if the measurements are not equal.

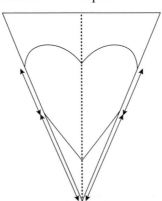

Once the master wedge is complete, draw over the pencil lines with a black pen or fine-tip marker to make the lines more visible for tracing.

Reverse Master Wedge – Nonsymmetrical Designs

When working with nonsymmetrical designs, there will be occasions when a *reverse* master wedge is required. The simplest way to create this is to redraw the master wedge on the other side of the paper. Turn the page over, and you should be able to see the lines clearly enough to draw right over them. Mark this side "reverse."

 Resizing a Sewflake

Sometimes the only thing wrong with a sewflake is its size. Rather than trying to recreate the design with a different size of paper sewflake, just resize the master wedge. Using a photocopier or a scanner, enlarge or reduce the master wedge to the desired size.

Transferring the Master Wedge to Template Material

Regardless of which appliqué method you use, the design will need to be transferred from the master wedge to the appropriate template material, such as freezer paper, fusible web, or water-soluble stabilizer. Specific instructions for each appliqué method can be found in Sewing Sewflakes, pages 19–21, but the transfer instructions remain the same.

Cut a square of template material—freezer paper, fusible web, or water-soluble stabilizer—the same size as the block. Use a ruler to draw registration lines for the type of wedge you are using. Mark on the non-shiny side of freezer paper and the paper side of fusible web. Use a water-soluble marker when working on water-soluble stabilizer.

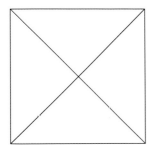

Registration lines for 30°, 45°, or 90° wedges

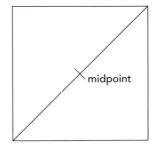

Registration lines for 60° wedges

 Wider Template Material

Template materials are available in different widths, yet you may still need a greater width for some sewflake designs. To make a piece of template material wider, join two strips together to make one larger piece. Freezer-paper strips can be fused together, or tape can be used on the paper side of fusible web.

SYMMETRICAL DESIGNS

Lay the template material on top of the master wedge, aligning the tip of the wedge with the center and one edge of the wedge with a registration line. Trace the design. Move the master wedge around to the next registration line and trace again, this time aligning with the previous tracing as well as with the center and registration line. Continue tracing the design from the master wedge until the entire sewflake design is complete.

For 45° wedges—Trace the master wedge 8 times.

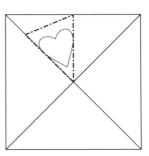

45° wedge, first trace

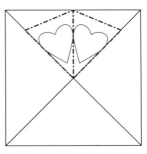

45° wedge, second trace

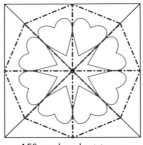

45° wedge, last trace

For 30° wedges—Trace the master wedge 12 times. Every third tracing will be aligned with the center and previous tracings only.

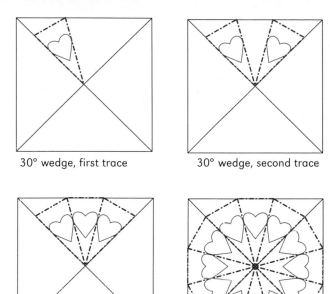

30° wedge, first trace

30° wedge, second trace

30° wedge, third trace

30° wedge, last trace

For 90° wedges—Trace the master wedge 4 times.
For 60° wedges—Trace the master wedge 6 times. Every third tracing will be aligned with the center and previous tracings only.

Aligned Designs

Even with a perfectly drawn and carefully measured master wedge, there will be times when the sewflake motifs don't line up exactly as they are traced onto the template material. Don't fret; just make slight adjustments at each intersection to bring the design back in line.

NONSYMMETRICAL DESIGNS

There are two types of nonsymmetrical designs: those that are nonsymmetrical within the wedge only and those that are completely nonsymmetrical. These two types of designs will be transferred in different ways.

Another important consideration when working with nonsymmetrical designs is the appliqué method. Some methods require the template material to be applied to the *wrong side* of the fabric, which will reverse the image when viewed from the right side. *In these cases, be sure to use a reverse master wedge for tracing.*

Nonsymmetrical within the wedge

The Sew Business sewflake, page 32, from the quilt *Tools of the Trade*, has the nonsymmetrical image of a sewing machine within the wedge, but the rest of the design is symmetrical. The lines that touch the edge of the wedge are the same on both sides.

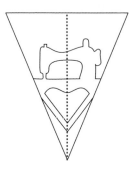

Sew Business wedge

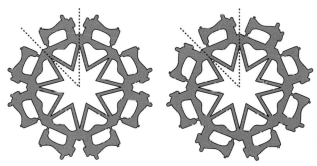

Sew Business sewflake

When I unfolded this paper sewflake, every other sewing machine was oriented in the opposite direction. But because the lines that touch the edges are the same, I can transfer this design to the template material in the same manner as a symmetrical design and keep each sewing machine oriented in the same direction. Remember to use a reverse master wedge for appliqué methods in which the template material is applied to the back of the fabric.

If I wanted to sew the block so that the sewing machines alternated their orientation, as they did in the paper sewflake, then I would transfer the design to the template material as if it were completely nonsymmetrical.

Completely nonsymmetrical

The Measure Up sewflake, page 33, from the quilt *Tools of the Trade*, is completely nonsymmetrical. The lines *do not* touch the sides of the wedge in the same place on the edges. Completely nonsymmetrical designs require a reverse master wedge.

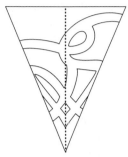 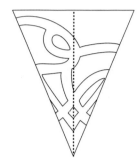

Measure Up wedge   Measure Up reverse wedge

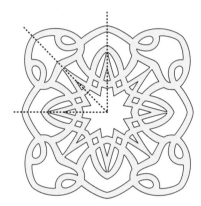

Measure Up sewflake

To trace a completely nonsymmetrical design onto template material, alternate tracing the master wedge with tracing the *reverse* master wedge.

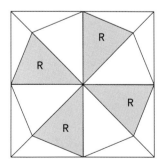 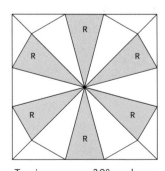

Tracing reverse 45° wedges   Tracing reverse 30° wedges

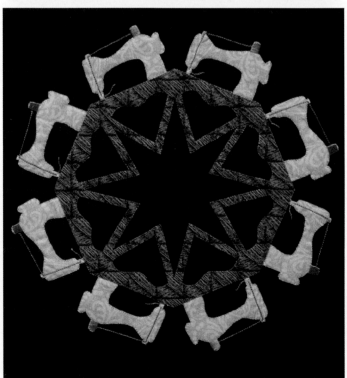

Sewing Sewflakes

The art of appliqué offers several methods. Sometimes the design dictates which appliqué method to use. Other times, your choice of appliqué method will influence your design. For example, a design like Pressing Matters, page 32, from the quilt *Tools of the Trade*, with its sharp points and tiny cutouts, might prove challenging with hand appliqué methods but can easily be managed with fusible web.

If you're intent on using hand appliqué, you may prefer softer points and gentler curves, such as those found in the fish in Catch of the Day, page 51, from the quilt *Go Fish*.

Freezer-Paper Appliqué

Freezer paper is often used as a template material for both hand and machine appliqué. It is applied to the *wrong* side of the fabric, so *the design will be reversed.*

Carefully cut out the traced design from the freezer paper. Iron the freezer paper sewflake, shiny side down, onto the *wrong* side of the appliqué fabric. Trim the appliqué fabric ¼˝ away from the edges of the freezer paper, clipping curves and inside points.

Prepare fabric with freezer paper.

Turn under the seam allowances and baste them to the freezer paper. A small dab of glue at tight inside points will help hold tiny threads in place.

Thread buste.

Pin or thread-baste the prepared appliqué onto the background fabric, matching the centers. Sew the appliqué to the background by hand or by machine, as described below.

HAND APPLIQUÉ

Use an appliqué needle and thread that matches the appliqué fabric (photo shown with contrasting thread for easy visibility). Use a blindstitch to appliqué the design to the background fabric. Bring the needle up through the background fabric, catching just a couple of threads in the fold of the appliqué edge. Insert the needle into the background fabric next to the last stitch and come up again into the appliqué fold.

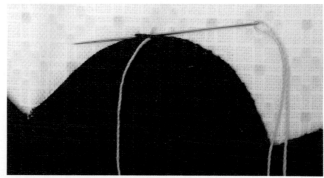
Hand appliqué stitch

MACHINE APPLIQUÉ

Set your sewing machine stitch to the blind stitch. It looks like several straight stitches followed by a zigzag stitch. Adjust the stitch width so it is just wide enough to catch the appliqué fabric with the zigzag.

Thread the machine with invisible monofilament thread in the needle and cotton thread in the bobbin. Using an appliqué presser foot, stitch the appliqué design to the background fabric.

Once the hand or machine appliqué is completed, remove the freezer paper by carefully cutting away the background fabric and then gently pulling the paper away.

Remove freezer paper.

Needle-Turn Appliqué

I prefer this method of hand appliqué because it saves time by eliminating the need to baste. The seam allowance is turned under with the tip of the needle as you sew. The design, however, is best transferred to *both* the appliqué fabric and the background fabric. To do this, rather than trying to trace through the fabric, I use freezer paper as my template material.

Cut out the traced design from the freezer paper, but iron the freezer-paper sewflake to the *right* side of the appliqué fabric. *Designs will not be reversed.* Trace around the outside edge of the freezer-paper template using a pencil or fine-tip fabric marker that is visible on the fabric. Carefully remove the freezer paper from the appliqué fabric, and reapply it to the right side of the background fabric, matching the centers. Trace again and remove the freezer paper.

Trace designs for needle-turn appliqué.

Trim the appliqué fabric a scant $1/4''$ from the marked edges of the design, clipping curves and inside points. Align the appliqué design with the marked background and pin or thread baste. Turn under a small portion of the seam allowance, and blindstitch the appliqué design to the background fabric as before. Continue to turn under small amounts of the seam allowance as you sew.

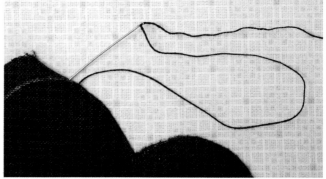

Hand stitching needle-turn appliqué

Fusible Appliqué

This method is quick and easy enough for beginners just learning to appliqué. It uses fusible web as the template material. Fusible web allows the appliqué design to be ironed onto the background fabric. *Designs will be reversed with this method*, as the template material is applied to the wrong side of the fabric.

Rough cut around the edges of the traced design on the fusible web. *Do not cut the traced lines at this point.* Place the paper side up on the wrong side of the appliqué fabric and fuse according to the manufacturer's directions. Cut out the appliqué design along the traced lines.

Some brands of fusible web have paper on *both* sides. If this is the kind you are using, carefully remove the paper side without the tracing before fusing the template to fabric.

Carefully remove the paper backing of the fusible web from the appliqué design. Arrange the appliqué onto the background fabric, aligning the centers, and fuse in place, following the manufacturer's directions.

Fuse appliqué to background.

FINISHING

To finish the raw edges of the appliqué, there are a number of options.

Hidden stitching—For a less obvious finished edge, stitch around the edges of the appliqué using a narrow zigzag stitch and invisible monofilament thread.

Decorative stitching—To highlight the finished edge, use machine embroidery thread and stitch around the edges of the appliqué with a satin stitch, a blanket stitch, or another decorative stitch.

For best results, place lightweight stabilizer on the wrong side of the appliquéd block when stitching the fusible appliqué edges.

Cutwork Appliqué

This method works well with negative image designs that have a lot of intricate cutouts. Clear, water-soluble stabilizer is used as the template material. It is applied to the right side of the fabric, so designs are *not* reversed.

After you have traced your design onto the water-soluble stabilizer, lay the stabilizer on the appliqué fabric and pin baste. Using cotton thread the same color as the appliqué fabric, machine stitch along the traced lines.

Outline stitch for cutwork appliqué.

From the fabric side, carefully cut away the excess fabric as close to the stitching as possible, leaving the stabilizer uncut.

Cut away excess fabric.

Matching the centers, lay the trimmed appliqué fabric, stabilizer side up, onto the background fabric, and pin baste. Satin stitch the raw edges of the design, using machine embroidery thread in a matching or contrasting color. I recommend using a hoop to further stabilize the stitching.

Satin stitch raw edges.

Trim away any large sections of stabilizer. Remove the remaining stabilizer by soaking the finished work in water, as directed by the manufacturer.

Creating Special Effects

The images within a sewflake are essentially silhouettes. While they may be hidden or not immediately obvious, the goal is to make them recognizable. Sometimes this means adding a little detail to the design.

Consider the Pins and Needles sewflake, page 31, from the quilt *Tools of the Trade*. When the thimble appears in the same fabric as the pincushion, it is hard to discern. Without the seamlines in the pincushion and the stitched pins and needles, the viewer might not recognize this image at all.

 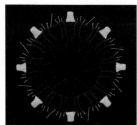

Pins and Needles sewflake
before embellishing

Pins and Needles sewflake
after embellishing

Even images that are recognizable can benefit from adding a bit of detail. Be creative, and see what you can come up with to embellish your design. Here are just a few ideas to get you started.

Multiple Fabrics

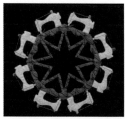

Instead of sewing the entire design from one single piece of fabric, change fabric to highlight a particular element. In the design Sew Business, page 32, from the quilt *Tools of the Trade*, the sewing machine is cut from a different fabric than the base. The fins in the Catch of the Day sewflake, page 51, from the quilt *Go Fish*, are highlighted by fussy-cutting a second fabric.

Sew Business sewflake

Embroidery

A little embroidery can go a long way toward enhancing your design. The pins, needle, and thread

in Pins and Needles, page 31, and the inch lines in Measure Up, page 33, both from the quilt *Tools of the Trade*, are important embroidered details!

 Tip The entire sewflake design can even be embroidered. My Valentine, stitched as an embroidery motif, looks like a redwork-style design.

Bias Strips

Very narrow elements in a design can be appliquéd separately using bias strips. Cut fabric strips on the bias three times the desired width. Using a little spray fabric starch, press one-third of the width to the wrong side, then press the remaining raw edge over to meet the fold. Bias strips were used to create the cherry stems in the Cherries Jubilee sewflake.

Cherries Jubilee
sewflake

Appliqué

Other elements can be appliquéd onto or around your design. The rotary cutter in The Cutting Edge sewflake is more recognizable with a blade and screw appliquéd onto it.

The Cutting Edge sewflake

In the design The House of the Lord, a heart appliquéd over the stairs conveys the idea of love following us "all the days of our lives."

House of the Lord
sewflake

Unique Elements

Measure Up sewflake

Mix things up a bit by changing one or two of the wedges in the sewflake. One apple in a sewflake design could have a bite taken out of it or a worm peeping out. In the design Measure Up, page 33, from the quilt *Tools of the Trade*, two wedges were altered to include the ends of the tape measure. To add a unique element, simply draw in the change after the master wedges have been traced onto the template material.

Buttons and Beads

Add detail to your design by embellishing it with buttons or beads. The fish eyes in Catch of the Day, page 51, from the quilt *Go Fish*, were created with a sequin and a seed bead. Seed beads were also used to represent the vent holes in the Pressing Matters irons. The hinge screw in the scissors from the Cut It Out sewflake is actually a snap!

Pressing Matters sewflake

Cut It Out sewflake

Quilting

Quilting adds texture, which could be just the detail that your design requires. The fish scales in the Catch of the Day sewflake are depicted in this way.

Catch of the Day sewflake

Fish scales

Sewflakes also make great quilting designs, especially with a little trapunto added.

Layering

While sewflakes can certainly stand alone, layering them can create some interesting effects. In the quilt *Go Fish*, page 46, the fish are appliquéd over a "net" of tulle. In the quilt *Fruitful*, (you can view the full quilt on my website at www.kathykwylie.com), five fruit sewflakes in various sizes are layered onto the Fruit Plate design. Outer sewflake designs can be layered like a series of borders.

Fruitful medallion

Cherries Jubilee sewflake

Banana Split sewflake

Plum Pudding sewflake

Poire Helene sewflake

Apple Pie sewflake

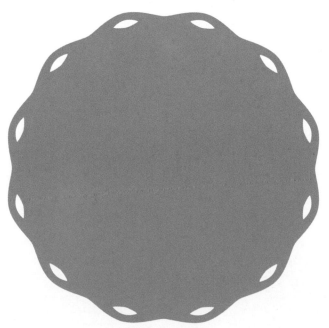

Fruit Plate sewflake

Pairing Sewflakes With Patchwork

What will you do with all your lovely sewflake designs? Will they stand alone, like a Hawaiian quilt, or go into a Baltimore Album–style quilt? I really like the look of appliqué with patchwork, and all the quilts in this book pair sewflakes with pieced blocks. I find that the appliqué softens the patchwork, and that patchwork provides a strong framework for the appliqué. Patchwork blocks can also add some extra color to what may otherwise be a two-color composition. But the real benefit of combining sewflakes with patchwork, to me, is the opportunity to communicate a theme in a subtle yet creative way.

Once you have the appliqué designed and the blocks chosen, consider how to put them together. The five sample layouts shown here give you examples of ways to pair sewflakes with patchwork.

Alternating Appliqué and Patchwork—Straight Set

For an easy and straightforward approach, simply alternate sewflake blocks with patchwork blocks. An uneven number of blocks works best for this layout. *King of Hearts*, page 58, is laid out essentially this way, with four sewflake blocks and five patchwork blocks.

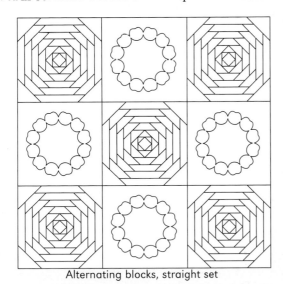

Alternating blocks, straight set

Alternating Appliqué and Patchwork—Set on Point

Setting the patchwork blocks on-point creates openings that are perfect for sewflakes. *The Lord Is My Shepherd*, page 34, is a good example of this layout.

Alternating blocks, set on point

Surrounding Appliqué with Patchwork

Patchwork blocks surrounding multiple sewflake blocks form a sashing, as in the quilt *Tools of the Trade*, page 27. They can also surround a single sewflake as a border, as in the quilt *Go Fish*, page 46.

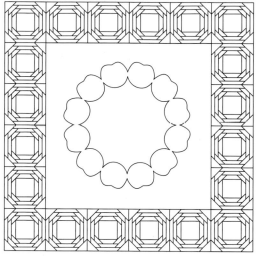

Surrounding appliqué with patchwork

Surrounding Patchwork with Appliqué

Sewflake blocks can also surround patchwork blocks. Outer sewflake designs work particularly well to frame patchwork blocks and create a sashing or a border. This layout is used in the quilt *Bridal Tea*, page 53.

Surrounding patchwork with appliqué

Appliqué on Patchwork

Some blocks contain enough open space or can be modified to allow the sewflake to be appliquéd right onto the block.

Appliqué on patchwork

Tools of the Trade

47¾″ × 64″, 2006, Kathy K. Wylie

Tools of the Trade takes a lighthearted look at the favorite tools in a quiltmaker's studio: thimble, pincushion, pins, and needles, rotary cutter and ruler, iron and ironing board, sewing machine, measuring tape, and scissors. These tools help make our quiltmaking successful. I think it's the same in life. Without the right tools, such as love, joy, peace, patience, kindness, goodness, faithfulness, gentleness, and self-control, it's hard to do a good job.

Fabric Requirements

Based on 40″ fabric width.

DESCRIPTION	EXAMPLE	YARDS	METERS
Background fabric	Black	$2^2/_3$	2.50
Spool fabric	Light brown	$^1/_2$	0.50
Accent border strip	Red	$^1/_4$	0.25
Outer border	Spools print	2	1.80
Binding	Blue	$^1/_2$	0.50
Thread fabric	Red, green, yellow, blue	Assorted scraps	

SEWFLAKES FABRIC

Pins and Needles	Red	12″ × 12″	
The Cutting Edge	Yellow	12″ × 12″	
Pressing Matters	Green	12″ × 12″	
Sew Business	Blue	12″ × 12″	
Measure Up	Yellow	12″ × 12″	
Cut It Out	Red	12″ × 12″	
Optional details (thimble, rotary blade, iron, sewing machine, scissor blades)	Silver	Fat quarter	

Cutting Instructions

Unless otherwise noted, strips are cut across the width of the fabric.

	NUMBER OF STRIPS	WIDTH	FIRST CUT QUANTITY	FIRST CUT SIZE	SECOND CUT
BACKGROUND FABRIC					
Appliqué blocks	3	13½″	6	13½″ × 13½″	
Patch A	15	1¼″	480	1¼″ × 1¼″	
Patch C	10	2½″	160	2½″ × 2½″	In half diagonally
Border 1	6	1½″			
SPOOL FABRIC					
Patch B	5	2¾″	160	2¾″ × 1¼″	
ACCENT BORDER STRIP					
Border 2	6	1″			
OUTER BORDER (CUT FROM LENGTH OF FABRIC)					
Border 3	4	5″			
BINDING					
	6	2½″			
THREAD FABRIC					
Patch A			80	1¼″ × 1¼″	

Other Supplies

Template material (freezer paper, fusible web, or water-soluble stabilizer):
   Six 12″ × 12″ pieces for sewflakes
   Two 12″ × 12″ pieces for optional details
Embellishments as desired, such as embroidery thread, buttons, snaps, and seed beads

Assembly

SPOOL OF THREAD BLOCKS

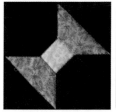 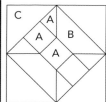

1. Sew a background Patch A to a thread Patch A. Press. Sew another background Patch A to the other side of the unit, as shown. Press. Unit Z should measure $1^1/_4″ \times 2^3/_4″$. Make 80, using different fabrics for thread Patch A.

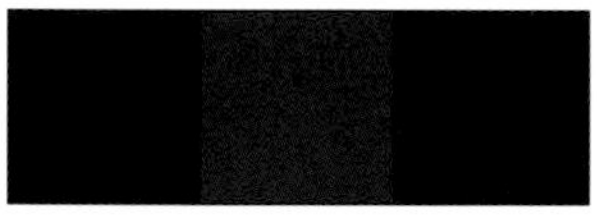

Unit Z; make 80.

2. Draw a diagonal line on the wrong sides of the remaining background A patches. Place a background Patch A on one end of a spool Patch B. Sew on the marked diagonal line.

3. Trim $^1/_4″$ away from the seam line. Press the background fabric toward the corner.

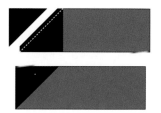

4. Sew another background Patch A to the unit, making sure the diagonal line runs in the opposite direction. Sew on the marked line.

5. Trim $1/4''$ away from the seam line. Press. Unit Y should measure $1^{1}/4'' \times 2^{3}/4''$. Make 160.

Unit Y; make 160.

6. Sew a Unit Y to a Unit Z, placing the narrow edge of the spool fabric toward the thread fabric as shown in Step 7. Press.

7. Sew another Unit Y to the other side of Unit Z, forming a YZY unit. Press. The unit should measure $2^{3}/4'' \times 2^{3}/4''$. Make 80.

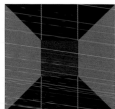

Unit YZY; make 80.

8. Sew a background Patch C to each side of this YZY unit to complete the Spool of Thread block. Press. The block should measure $3^{3}/4'' \times 3^{3}/4''$. Make 80.

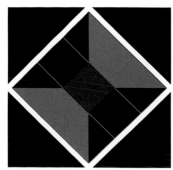

Spool of Thread block; make 80.

SEWFLAKE BLOCKS

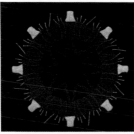

Pins and Needles block

The Cutting Edge block

Pressing Matters block

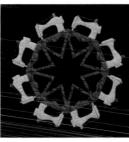

Sew Business block

Measure Up block

Cut It Out block

1. Using the *Tools of the Trade* patterns on pages 31–33, transfer each sewflake to a $12'' \times 12''$ square of the template material of your choice (see Preparing a Sewflake Pattern, pages 15–18). Keep the following in mind:

   a. Each sewflake in *Tools of the Trade* repeats the master wedge 8 times.

   b. Pressing Matters and Sew Business have nonsymmetrical images in their designs; be sure to use a reverse master wedge if you will be transferring the sewflake to the wrong side of the fabric.

   c. Measure Up is completely nonsymmetrical. For this block, trace 4 master wedges alternating with 4 reverse wedges.

2. Prepare sewflake fabrics according to the desired appliqué method (see Sewing Sewflakes, pages 19–21). I used fusible appliqué with hidden stitching for this quilt.

3. If you are changing fabric for the optional details, prepare the second fabric according to the desired appliqué method. Consult the individual block designs on pages 31–33 for specific instructions. For the block Cut It Out, the scissor blades can be cut as one piece from the silver sewflake fabric, and the 8 scissor handles can be cut from the contrasting fabric.

4. If 2 fabrics are being used, cut away elements from the sewflake fabric, as noted on the following chart.

BLOCK	CUT AWAY
Pins and Needles	Thimbles
Pressing Matters	Irons (plate view)
Sew Business	Sewing machines
Cut It Out	Scissor handles

Cut-away elements

5. Arrange the appliqué patches onto the background fabric so that the sewflake is centered, and appliqué it in place.

6. If desired, add embellishments to the block, as noted in the following chart.

BLOCK	EMBELLISHMENT
Pins and Needles	Embroider pin cushion seams, pins, needles and thread
The Cutting Edge	Embroider inch lines on rulers. Appliqué rotary cutter blades and screws.
Pressing Matters	Satin stitch edge of side-view irons Sew seed beads on plate-view irons
Sew Business	Satin stitch thread in spools Embroider thread going through needle
Measure Up	Embroider inch lines
Cut It Out	Sew on buttons or snaps for hinge screws

Sewflake embellishments

Sashing

1. For vertical sashing, arrange and sew 4 Spool of Thread blocks in a row, alternating the orientation of the spool in each block and consulting the assembly diagram for placement. Press. Vertical sashing strips should measure $3^3/4'' \times 13^1/2''$. Make 9 strips.

2. For horizontal sashing, arrange and sew 11 Spool of Thread blocks in a row, alternating the orientation of the spool in each block and consulting the assembly diagram for placement. Press. Horizontal sashing strips should measure $3^3/4'' \times 36^1/4''$. Make 4 strips.

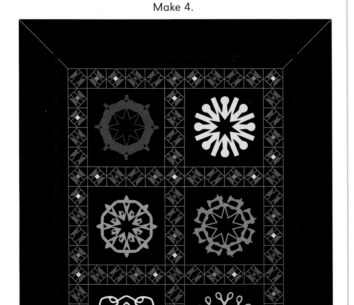

Make 4.

Make 9.

Tools of the Trade assembly diagram

Quilt Assembly

1. Consulting the assembly diagram below, sew 3 vertical sashing strips to 2 sewflake blocks to make a row. Press. Make 3.

2. Arrange and sew 4 horizontal sashing strips to the rows from Step 1. Press.

3. Join two $1^1/2''$ background strips end-to-end. Press. Make 2. Join two $1''$ accent border strips end to end. Press. Make 2.

4. For the horizontal borders on the top and the bottom, sew a short background border strip, a short accent border strip, and an outer border strip together, matching the centers. **Note:** Borders are various lengths. Press. For the vertical borders on the sides, sew a long background border strip, a long accent border strip, and an outer border strip together, matching the centers. Press.

5. Sew the border strip sets to all 4 sides of the quilt top, mitering the corners. Press.

6. Arrange backing, batting and quilt top together. Hand or machine quilt, as desired. Attach the binding.

PINS AND NEEDLES

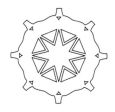

Optional details:
- Cut 8 thimbles from silver fabric.
- Embroider pincushion seams, pins, needles, and thread.

Line Guide

Tracing Line	————————
Guide Line	··················
Quilting/Embroidery Line	– – – – – – – –
Placement Line	–·–··–··–··–··–··–··

THE CUTTING EDGE

Optional details:
- Cut 8 rotary cutter blades from silver fabric.
- Cut 8 rotary cutter centers from black fabric.
- Embroider inch lines on the rulers.

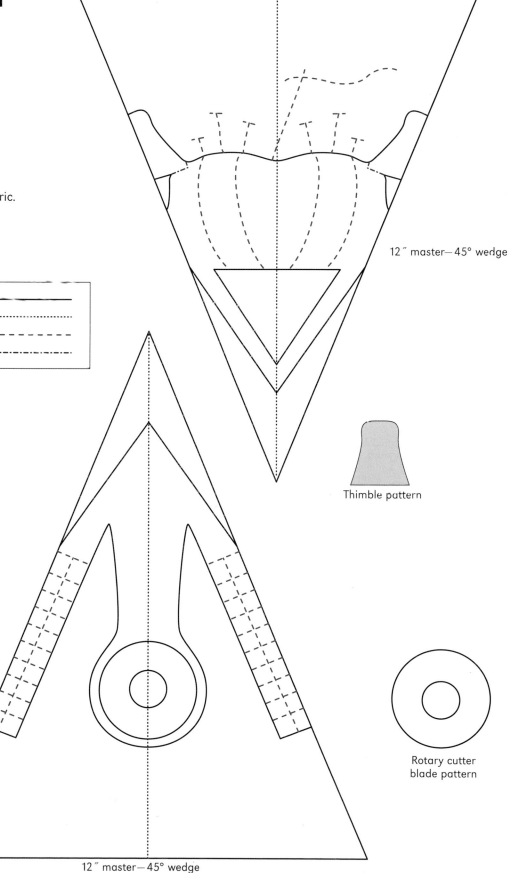

12″ master—45° wedge

Thimble pattern

Rotary cutter blade pattern

12″ master—45° wedge

PRESSING MATTERS

Optional details:
- Cut 8 irons from silver fabric.
- Satin stitch the edge of the side-view irons.
- Sew seed beads on the plate-view irons.

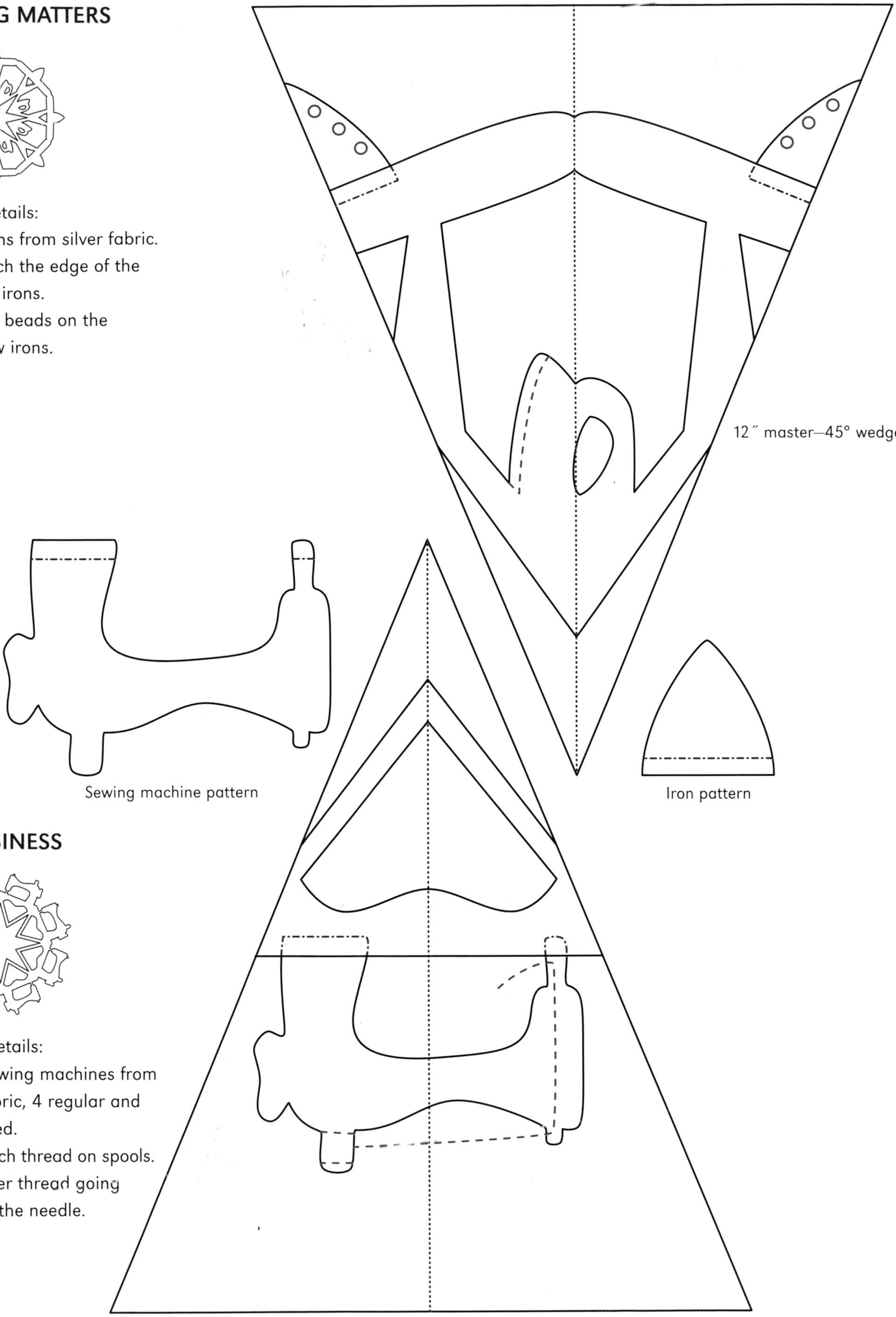

12″ master—45° wedge

Sewing machine pattern

Iron pattern

SEW BUSINESS

Optional details:
- Cut 8 sewing machines from silver fabric, 4 regular and 4 reversed.
- Satin stitch thread on spools.
- Embroider thread going through the needle.

12″ master—45° wedge

MEASURE UP

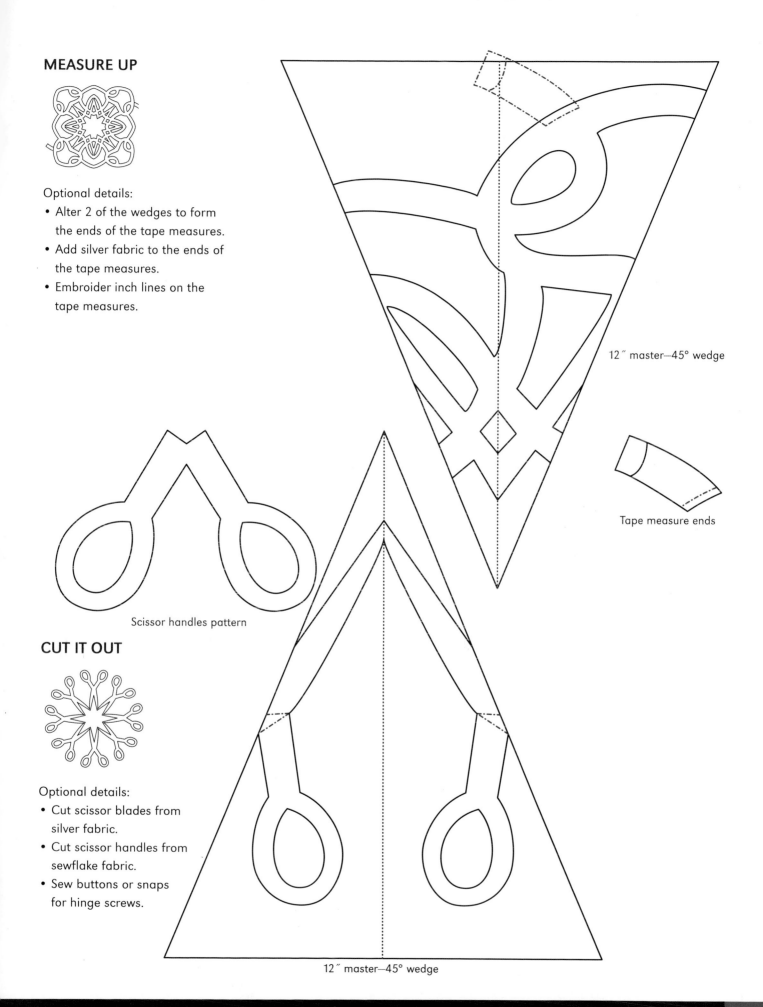

Optional details:

- Alter 2 of the wedges to form the ends of the tape measures.
- Add silver fabric to the ends of the tape measures.
- Embroider inch lines on the tape measures.

Scissor handles pattern

CUT IT OUT

Optional details:

- Cut scissor blades from silver fabric.
- Cut scissor handles from sewflake fabric.
- Sew buttons or snaps for hinge screws.

12″ master—45° wedge

Tape measure ends

12″ master—45° wedge

The Lord Is My Shepherd

68″ × 68″, 2003, Kathy K. Wylie

The design for this quilt originated with the discovery of a block named Shepherd's Light.
I developed the shepherd theme by incorporating imagery from the 23rd Psalm—green
pastures and still waters, rod and staff, a table prepared before me, the house of the
Lord, my cup overflowing. Jesus said, "I am the good shepherd. The good shepherd lays
down his life for the sheep." The Lord is my shepherd. His Spirit is my strength.

Fabric Requirements

Based on 40″ fabric width.

DESCRIPTION	EXAMPLE	YARDS	METERS
Background fabric	Pale yellow	$3\frac{5}{8}$	3.20
Border fabric	Dark green	$1\frac{7}{8}$	1.60

The 16-Patch units contain 7 fabrics that gradually transition from the yellow background fabric to the dark green border fabric. These fabrics are numbered such that Fabric 1 is the lightest and Fabric 7 is the darkest. Fabric 2 is also used to form the cross in the background, and Fabric 7 is used for the sewflakes and the small star points.

Fabric 1	Light yellow	$\frac{1}{4}$	0.25
Fabric 2	↓	1	0.90
Fabric 3	↓	$\frac{1}{2}$	0.50
Fabric 4	↓	$\frac{7}{8}$	0.80
Fabric 5	↓	$\frac{3}{4}$	0.70
Fabric 6	↓	$\frac{5}{8}$	0.60
Fabric 7	Dark green	$1\frac{3}{8}$	1.30

Cutting Instructions

Unless otherwise noted, strips are cut across the width of the fabric.

	NUMBER OF STRIPS	WIDTH	FIRST CUT QUANTITY	FIRST CUT SIZE	SECOND CUT
BACKGROUND FABRIC					
Patch A	12	$3\frac{1}{2}''$	72	$3\frac{1}{2}'' \times 6''$	Using template A
Patch C	1	$4''$	9	$4'' \times 4''$	Using template C
Setting squares	1	$12\frac{1}{2}''$	2	$12\frac{1}{2}'' \times 12\frac{1}{2}''$	
Setting squares	1	$6\frac{1}{2}''$	4	$6\frac{1}{2}'' \times 6\frac{1}{2}''$	
Setting triangles	1	$18\frac{1}{4}''$	2	$18\frac{1}{4}'' \times 18\frac{1}{4}''$	In quarters diagonally
Corner triangles	1	$9\frac{3}{8}''$	2	$9\frac{3}{8}'' \times 9\frac{3}{8}''$	In half diagonally
Border 2	6	$2''$			
Border 3 triangles	2	$6\frac{1}{4}''$	11	$6\frac{1}{4}'' \times 6\frac{1}{4}''$	In quarters diagonally
			2	$3\frac{3}{8}'' \times 3\frac{3}{8}''$	In half diagonally
BORDER FABRIC					
Border 1	6	$1''$			
Border 3 triangles	2	$6\frac{1}{4}''$	11	$6\frac{1}{4}'' \times 6\frac{1}{4}''$	In quarters diagonally
Border 3 triangles	1	$3\frac{3}{8}''$	6	$3\frac{3}{8}'' \times 3\frac{3}{8}''$	In half diagonally
Border 4	8	$2''$			
Binding	8	$2\frac{1}{2}''$			
FABRIC 1					
16-Patch units	3	$1\frac{3}{8}''$			
FABRIC 2					
16-Patch units	6	$1\frac{3}{8}''$			
Setting squares	1	$12\frac{1}{2}''$	2	$12\frac{1}{2}'' \times 12\frac{1}{2}''$	
Setting squares	1	$6\frac{7}{8}''$	2	$6\frac{7}{8}'' \times 6\frac{7}{8}''$	In half diagonally
			2	$6\frac{1}{2}'' \times 6\frac{1}{2}''$	
FABRIC 3					
16-Patch units	10	$1\frac{3}{8}''$			
FABRIC 4					
16-Patch units	14	$1\frac{3}{8}''$			
16-Patch units	3	$2\frac{1}{2}''$	36	$2\frac{1}{2}'' \times 2\frac{1}{2}''$	In quarters diagonally
FABRIC 5					
16-Patch units	17	$1\frac{3}{8}''$			
FABRIC 6					
16-Patch units	12	$1\frac{3}{8}''$			
FABRIC 7					
16-Patch units	6	$1\frac{3}{8}''$			
Patch B	4	$3''$	72	$3'' \times 2''$	Using template B
Sewflakes	2	$12''$	4	$12'' \times 12''$	

Other Supplies

Template material (freezer paper, fusible web, or water-soluble stabilizer):

    Four 10″ × 10″ pieces for sewflakes

    Nine 4″ × 4″ pieces for Patch C

Block Assembly

SHEPHERD'S LIGHT BLOCKS

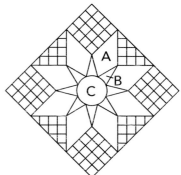

16-Patch Units

1. Sew a $1\frac{3}{8}''$ strip from Fabrics 1, 2, 3, and 4 together. Press. Make 3. From these strip sets, cut eighty $1\frac{3}{8}''$-wide segments. The unit measures $1\frac{3}{8}'' \times 4''$.

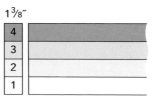

Make 3. Cut 80 segments.

2. Sew a 1³/₈″ strip from Fabrics 2, 3, 4, and 5 together. Press. Make 3. From these strip sets, cut eighty 1³/₈″-wide segments. The unit measures 1³/₈″ × 4″.

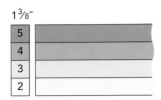

Make 3. Cut 80 segments.

3. Sew a 1³/₈″ strip from Fabrics 3, 4, 5, and 6 together. Press. Make 4. From these strip sets, cut eighty-eight 1³/₈″-wide segments. The unit measures 1³/₈″ × 4″.

Make 4. Cut 88 segments.

4. Sew a 1³/₈″ strip from Fabrics 4, 5, 6, and 7 together. Press. Make 4. From these strip sets, cut eighty-eight 1³/₈″-wide segments. The unit measures 1³/₈″ × 4″.

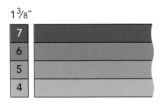

Make 4. Cut 88 segments.

5. Sew 1 of each strip set from Steps 1–4 together to form a 16- Patch unit. Press. The unit should measure 4″ × 4″. Make 80.

Make 80.

6. Referring to the diagram, arrange and sew together the remaining strip sets from Steps 3 and 4 to make four 16-Patch units for the Border 3 corners. Press. Make 4.

Make 4.

Triangles

1. Sew a 1³/₈″ strip from Fabrics 5, 6, and 7 together. Press. Make 2. From these strip sets, cut thirty-six 1³/₈″-wide segments. The unit measures 1³/₈″ × 3¹/₈″.

Make 2. Cut 36 segments.

2. Sew a 1³/₈″ strip from Fabrics 5 and 6 together. Press. Make 2. From these strip sets, cut thirty-six 1³/₈″-wide segments. The unit measures 1³/₈″ × 2¹/₄″.

Make 2. Cut 36 segments.

3. From the remaining 1³/₈″ strips of Fabric 5, cut 36 squares 1³/₈″ × 1³/₈″.

4. Sew a Fabric 4 triangle onto each Fabric 5 square, the single squares from Step 3, as well as the strip sets from Steps 1 and 2. Press.

5. Join 1 of each of these strips together with the remaining Fabric 4 triangles to form the triangle units. Press. Make 36.

Make 36.

Joining the Units

1. Sew a background Patch A to a Fabric 7 Patch B. Press. Make 72.

AB Unit
Make 72.

2. Sew 2 AB units from Step 1 together. Press. Make 36.

Make 36.

3. Set in a pieced triangle unit as follows: sew one short side of the triangle to the long edge of a Patch A, backstitching at the AB seam and *not* stitching into the seam allowance. Align the other short edge of the triangle with the second Patch A, and stitch, again backstitching at the AB seam. Press. Make 36.

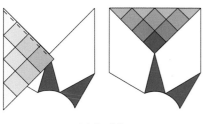

Make 36.

4. Referring to the Step 5 diagram, sew 2 of these units together. Press. Make 18.

5. Set in one 16-Patch square to a unit from Step 4, making sure that Fabric 7 is in the inside corner. Press. Make 18.

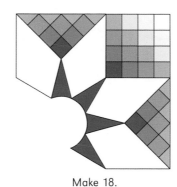

Make 18.

6. Sew units from Step 5 together in pairs and press. Sew two 16-Patch units to each unit. Press. Make 9.

Make 9.

7. Appliqué a background Patch C over the center opening of the block. The completed block should measure $12\frac{1}{2}'' \times 12\frac{1}{2}''$.

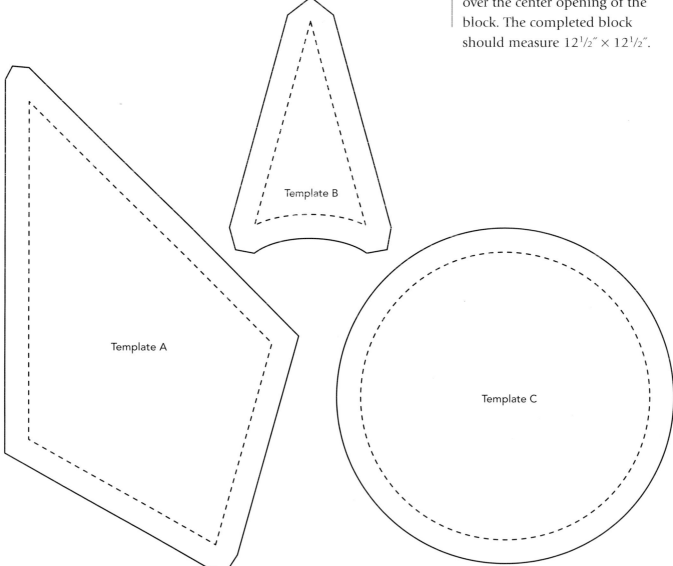

Template A

Template B

Template C

BACKGROUND BLOCKS

1. On the wrong side of each $6\frac{1}{2}'' \times 6\frac{1}{2}''$ background setting square and Fabric 2 setting square, draw a diagonal line from corner to corner.

2. Place 1 marked Fabric 2 $6\frac{1}{2}''$ setting square on one corner of a background $12\frac{1}{2}''$ setting square, right sides together, so that the diagonal line crosses the corner. Stitch on the marked line. Trim $\frac{1}{4}''$ from the sewn line. Press the Fabric 2 triangle away from the background. Make 2.

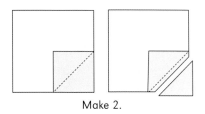

Make 2.

3. Refer to Step 2 to sew, trim, and press 2 background $6\frac{1}{2}''$ setting squares on the opposite corners of one $12\frac{1}{2}''$ Fabric 2 setting square. Make 2.

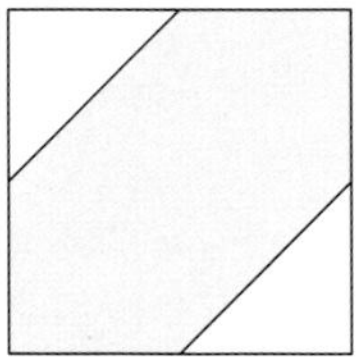

Make 2.

4. On the wrong side of each $6\frac{7}{8}''$ Fabric 2 triangle, draw a line dividing the triangle in half.

5. Lay a $6\frac{7}{8}''$ Fabric 2 triangle on 1 corner of a large background setting triangle, right sides together. Stitch on the marked line. Make 4 (2 with the Fabric 2 triangle on the right and 2 with the Fabric 2 triangle on the left).

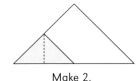 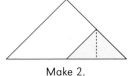

Make 2.   Make 2.

6. Trim $\frac{1}{4}''$ from the sewn line. Press the Fabric 2 triangle away from the background.

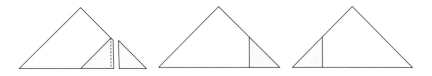

SEWFLAKE BLOCKS

House of the Lord block

A Table Prepared Before Me block

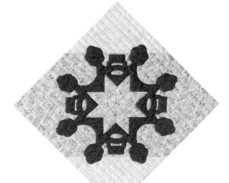

Green Pastures and Still Waters block

Rod and Staff block

1. Using the *Lord Is My Shepherd* patterns on pages 44–45, transfer each sewflake design to a 10″ × 10″ square of the template material of your choice (see Preparing a Sewflake Pattern, pages 15–18). Keep the following in mind:

a. Sewflakes for *The Lord Is My Shepherd* repeat the master wedge 4 times, and the 90° angle is formed horizontally and vertically rather than diagonally.

b. A Table Prepared Before Me has a nonsymmetrical image in the design; be sure to use a reverse master wedge if you will be transferring the sewflake to the wrong side of the fabric.

2. Prepare Fabric 7 according to the desired appliqué method. I used needle-turn hand appliqué for this quilt.

3. Center Green Pastures and Still Waters and Rod and Staff on the background blocks with Fabric 2 squares and background fabric triangles, and appliqué.

4. Center A Table Prepared Before Me and The House of the Lord on the background blocks with background fabric squares and a Fabric 2 triangle, and appliqué.

Quilt Assembly

Assemble the Shepherd's Light blocks, the appliquéd sewflake blocks, and the background setting and corner triangles in diagonal rows according to the assembly diagram.

The Lord Is My Shepherd assembly diagram

BORDERS 1 AND 2

1. Cut 2 of the 1″ border fabric Border 1 strips into two 20″ lengths. Trim the selvages from the remaining 4 strips, and sew a 20″ strip onto each. Press. The Border 1 strips should now be at least 60″ long.

2. Cut 2 of the 2″ background Border 2 strips into two 20″ lengths. Trim the selvages from the remaining 4 strips, and sew a 20″ strip onto each. Press. The Border 2 strips should now be at least 60″ long.

3. Sew the Border 1 and Border 2 strips together. Press. Sew these strips onto all 4 sides of the quilt top, mitering the corners. Press.

BORDER 3

1. Sew a large background Border 3 triangle to the Fabric 1/2/3/4 side of a 16-Patch unit as shown. Press. Make 42. Repeat this step to make 2 using two 16-Patch units for the Border 3 corners. Press.

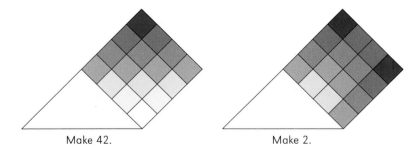

Make 42.　　　　Make 2.

2. To 40 of the 42 units, sew a large border fabric Border 3 triangle to the Fabric 4/5/6/7 side as shown.

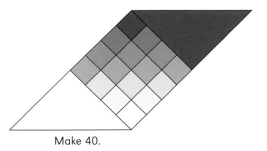

Make 40.

3. To 2 of the remaining units, sew a small border fabric triangle to the Fabric 4/5/6/7 side and a small background fabric triangle to the other Fabric 1/2/3/4 side as shown. Press. Make 2 with the corner 16-Patch unit and 2 small border fabric triangles. Press.

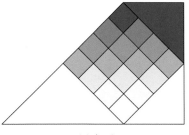

Make 2.   Make 2 (corner 16-Patch).

4. Using the final 2 regular 16-Patch units, sew a small background triangle to the Fabric 1/2/3/4 side and large and small border fabric triangles to the Fabric 4/5/6/7 sides. Press. Using the remaining 2 corner 16-Patch units, sew small border fabric triangles to one Fabric 4/5/6/7 side and the Fabric 7/6/6/7 side, and a large border fabric triangle to the other Fabric 4/5/6/7 side. Press.

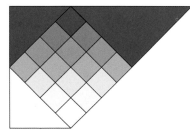

Make 2.   Make 2 (corner 16-Patch).

5. Sew 9 of the units from Step 2 together with a unit from Step 3 and a unit from Step 4 to form a side Border 3. Press. Make 2.

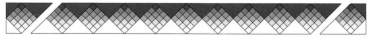

Make 2.

6. Referring to the layout, sew these borders to the sides of the quilt top, with the background triangles facing Border 2.

7. Sew 11 of the units from Step 2 together with a corner unit from Step 3 and a corner unit from Step 4 to form the rest of Border 3. Press. Make 2.

Make 2.

8. Sew these borders to the top and bottom of the quilt top, with the background triangles facing Border 2.

BORDER 4

1. Sew together 2 of the 2″ borders from Border 4 strips. The Border 4 strips should now measure at least 80″ long. Make 4.

2. Sew these strips onto all 4 sides of the quilt top, mitering the corners.

3. Arrange backing, batting and quilt top together. Hand or machine quilt, as desired. Attach the binding.

Quilting Tips

Quilt the My Cup Overflowing motif, pages 42–43, in the 8 large setting triangles. Quilt the My Head Anointed motif, page 43, in the 4 corner setting triangles.

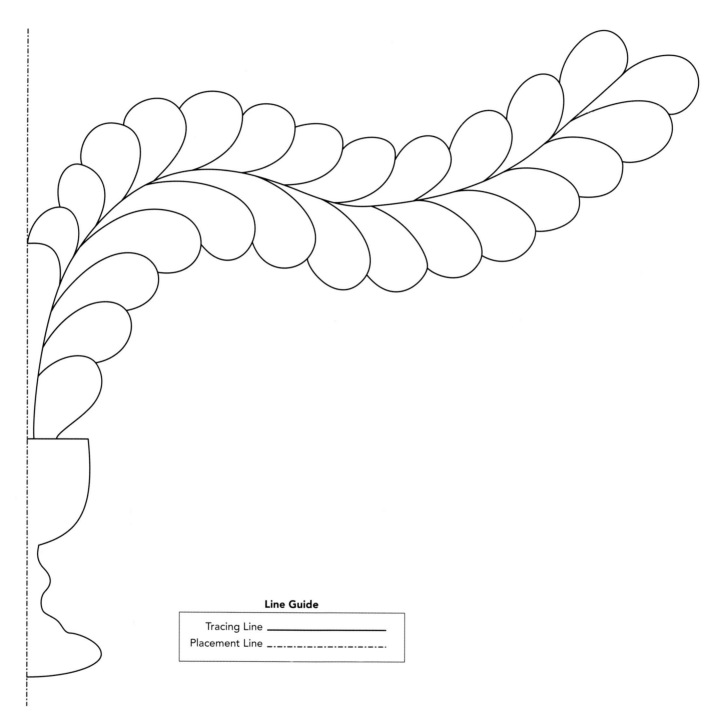

Line Guide

Tracing Line ——————

Placement Line _._._._._._._._._._._.

My Cup Overflowing quilting pattern 1

My Cup Overflowing quilting pattern 2

My Head Anointed quilting pattern

GREEN PASTURES
AND STILL WATERS

10˝ master—90° wedge

Line Guide

Tracing Line	————————
Guide Line	····················

ROD AND STAFF

10˝ master—90° wedge

A TABLE PREPARED BEFORE ME

THE HOUSE OF THE LORD

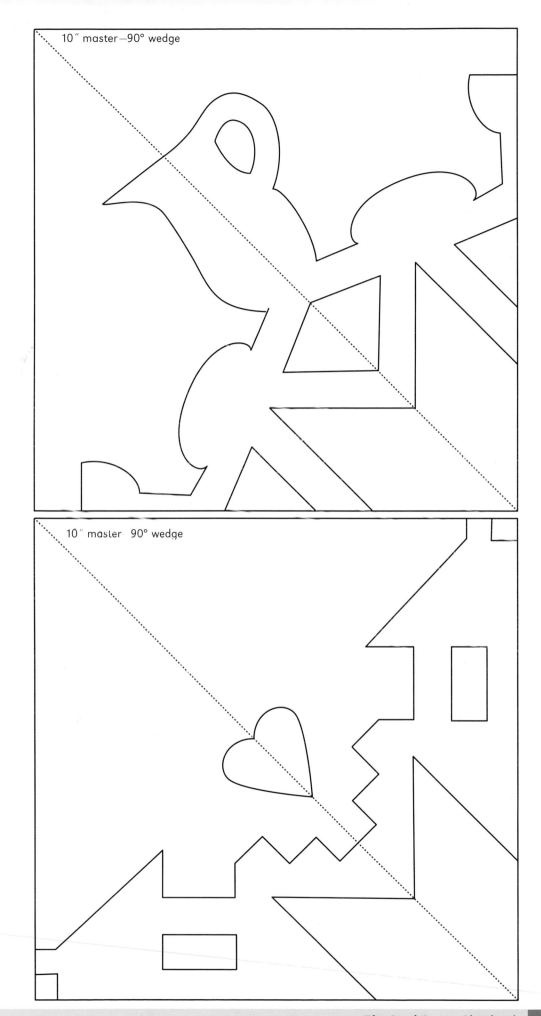

10″ master—90° wedge

10″ master—90° wedge

Go Fish

30″ × 30″, 2005, Kathy K. Wylie

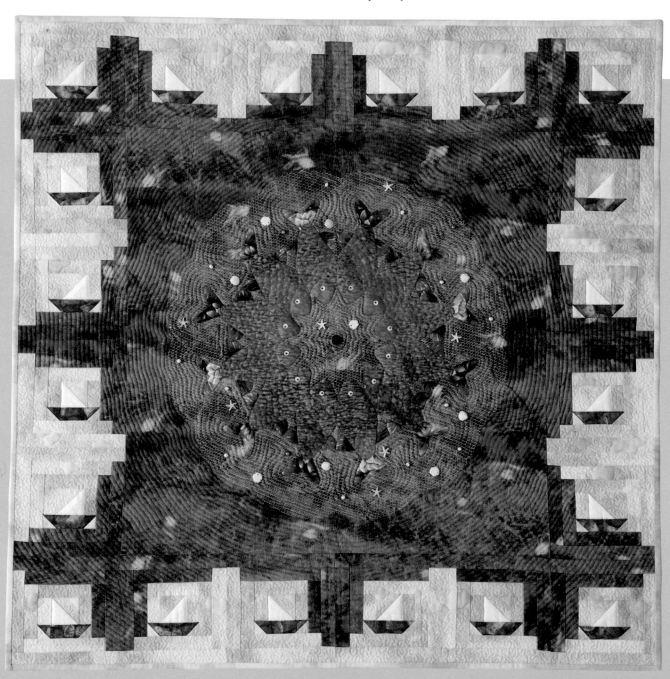

Go Fish is no ordinary fish story. It's the story of Simon, who had been fishing all night but hadn't caught a thing. The next morning, a man came along and suggested that Simon let down his nets one more time. Simon was puzzled. Why should he listen to this stranger? Simon could tell that the man didn't fish—in fact, he looked like a carpenter! But Simon agreed. "Because you say so, I will." Those words changed his life—and his name—forever. Simon let down his nets and caught so many fish that the nets began to break! So, when the man told Simon to "Go, fish" for men, Simon knew what he must do. He obeyed.

Fabric Requirements

Based on 40″ fabric width.

DESCRIPTION	EXAMPLE	YARDS	METERS
Background fabric	Blue water	1*	0.90*
Sky fabric	Blue sky	1*	0.90*
Sail fabric	White	⅛	0.10
Boat hull fabric	Brown	⅛	0.10
SEWFLAKES FABRIC			
Catch of the Day	Green	15″ × 15″	
Fish Net	Tulle	18″ × 18″	
Fish fins (optional)	Pink and green	Assorted scraps 12 @ 2½″ × 1¾″ 24 @ 1½″ × 1½″	

*For paper foundation piecing of the Log Cabin Boat blocks, add an extra ¼ yard or meter to these measurements.

Cutting Instructions

Unless otherwise noted, strips are cut across the width of the fabric.

The cutting instructions for Patches A to G are for traditional piecing of the Log Cabin Boat blocks. For paper foundation piecing, you may wish to cut the patches a little larger.

	NUMBER OF STRIPS	WIDTH	FIRST CUT QUANTITY	FIRST CUT SIZE	SECOND CUT
BACKGROUND FABRIC					
Center block	1	20½″	1	20½″ × 20½″	
Patch A	3	1⅛″	20	1⅛″ × 5½″	
Patch B	5	1⅛″	40	1⅛″ × 4¼″	
Patch C	2	1⅛″	20	1⅛″ × 3″	
SKY FABRIC					
Patch A	3	1⅛″	20	1⅛″ × 5½″	
Patch B	5	1⅛″	40	1⅛″ × 4¼″	
Patch C	4	1⅛″	40	1⅛″ × 3″	
Patch D	2	1⅛″	40	1⅛″ × 1⅛″	
Patch F	2	1⅛″	40	1⅛″ × 1¾″	
Patch G	1	2⅛″	10	2⅛″ × 2⅛″	In half diagonally
Binding	4	2¼″			
SAIL FABRIC					
Patch G	1	2⅛″	10	2⅛″ × 2⅛″	In half diagonally
BOAT HULL FABRIC					
Patch E	2	1⅛″	20	1⅛″ × 3″	

Other Supplies

Template material (freezer paper, fusible web, or water-soluble stabilizer):

One 15″ × 15″ piece for Catch of the Day sewflake

One 12″ × 12″ piece for fish fins (optional)

18″ × 18″ square of freezer paper for Fish Net sewflake

Sequins, seed beads, seashells, and pearls (optional)

Block Assembly

LOG CABIN BOAT BLOCKS

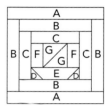

Traditional Piecing

1. Sew a sky Patch G to a sail Patch G. Press. Make 20.

Make 20.

2. Sew a sky Patch F to both sides of a unit from Step 1. Make 20 (10 with the sail toward the right and 10 with the sail toward the left).

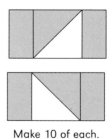

Make 10 of each.

3. Draw a diagonal line on the wrong side of each sky Patch D. Place a sky Patch D onto a boat hull Patch E, right sides together, and sew on the marked line. Trim ¼″ away from the stitching and press the triangle away from the boat hull. Repeat for the other side of boat hull Patch E, using the remaining sky D Patches. Press. Make 20.

Make 20.

4. Join the boat hull unit from Step 3 to the sail unit from Step 2. Press. Make 20 (10 of each variation).

 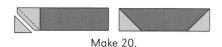

Boat 1; make 10. Boat 2; make 10.

5. Sew a sky Patch C to the top of each boat. Press. Make 20 (10 of each variation).

Boat 1; make 10. Boat 2; make 10.

6. Continue adding C patches, B patches, and A patches in Log Cabin style, according to the diagrams below. Press. Make 20 (5 of each variation). Completed blocks should measure 5½″ × 5½″.

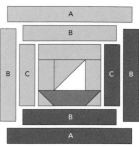

Log Cabin Boat block 1A; make 5.

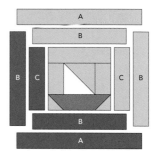

Log Cabin Boat block 2A; make 5.

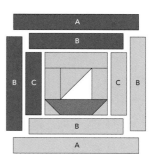

Log Cabin Boat block 1B; make 5.

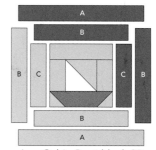

Log Cabin Boat block 2B; make 5.

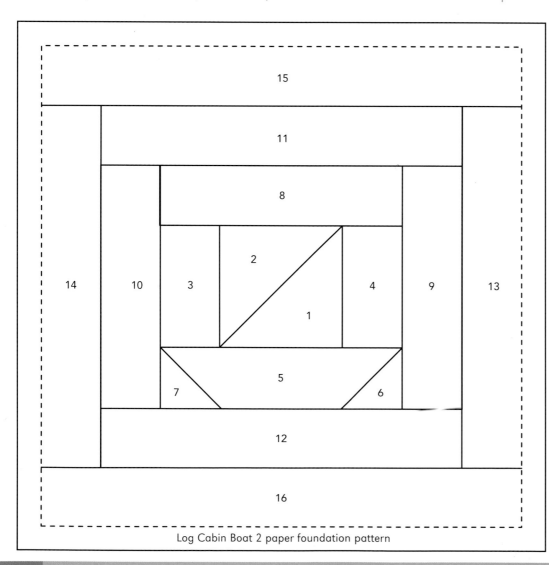

Log Cabin Boat 2 paper foundation pattern

Paper Foundation Piecing

1. For paper foundation piecing, make 10 copies each of the Log Cabin Boat 1 and Log Cabin Boat 2 patterns. Add patches in numerical sequence, consulting the traditional piecing diagrams. Paper piecing produces a mirror image of the pattern. Place fabrics accordingly.

2. Make 5 of blocks 1A, 1B, 2A, and 2B.

SEWFLAKE BLOCKS

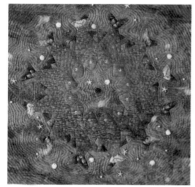

Go Fish block

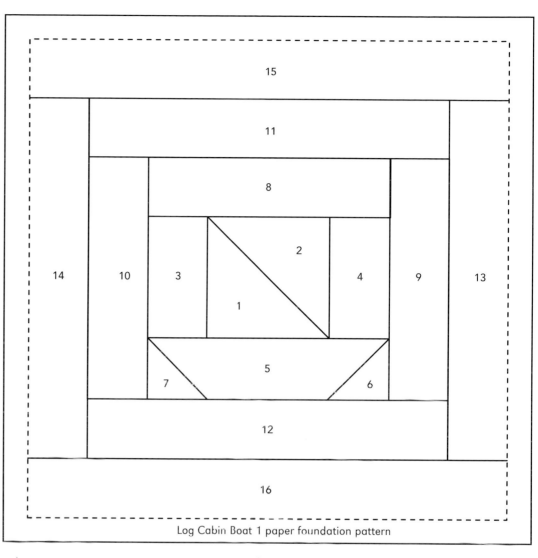

Log Cabin Boat 1 paper foundation pattern

1. Using the *Go Fish* patterns on pages 51–52, transfer the Catch of the Day sewflake from the master wedge to a 14˝ × 14˝ square of the template material of your choice (see Preparing a Sewflake Pattern, pages 15–18). Keep in mind that the *Go Fish* sewflakes repeat the master wedge 12 times and are symmetrical designs.

2. Transfer the Fish Net sewflake to an 18˝ × 18˝ square of freezer paper.

> **Note** See the tip on page 16 if the template material is not wide enough for the designs.

3. Pin the freezer paper Fish Net sewflake onto the tulle fabric. Use the freezer paper pattern to cut out a tulle Fish Net. Remove the freezer paper.

4. Center the tulle Fish Net onto the 20½˝ background block. Thread baste in place.

5. Prepare the Catch of the Day fabric according to the desired appliqué method. I used needle-turn hand appliqué for this quilt.

6. If you are using a separate fabric for the fish fins, prepare and appliqué the fins in place first, onto the tulle and background fabric together. Consult the Catch

of the Day master wedge for placement.

7. Appliqué the Catch of the Day sewflake over the fins and onto the tulle and background fabric together.

8. If desired for extra detail, embellish each fish using a sequin and a seed bead to create a fish eye.

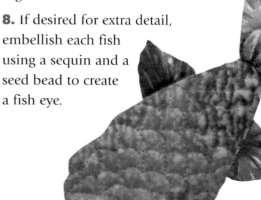

Quilt Assembly

1. For the top border, join a Log Cabin Boat block 2A, 1A, 2A, and 1A. Referring to the assembly diagram, sew this unit's background fabric edge to one edge of the background center block. Press.

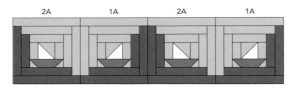

2. For the bottom border, join a Log Cabin Boat block 1B, 2B, 1B, and 2B. Sew the background fabric edge of this unit to the opposite edge of the background center block to form the bottom border. Press.

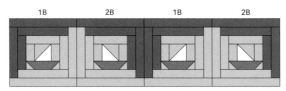

3. For the left side border, join a Log Cabin Boat block 1A, 2B, 1A, 2B, 1A, 2B. For the right side border, join a Log Cabin Boat block 2A, 1B, 2A, 1B, 2A, 1B. Sew these units to the left and right edges of the center block, keeping the border fabric edges toward the center. Press.

4. Arrange backing, batting and quilt top together. Hand or machine quilt, as desired. Attach the binding.

> **Tip** Remove the basting thread from the tulle Fish Net before quilting. The quilting stitches will hold the tulle in place. If desired, place seashell shapes or pearl-like beads under the tulle before quilting. To add detail, quilt scales on the fish and echo quilt around the fish to give the appearance of waves rippling in the water.

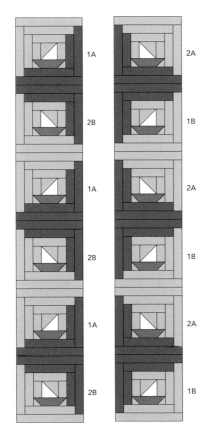

Go Fish assembly diagram

Go Fish
SEWFLAKE PATTERNS

To add extra details to the quilt, sew sequins and beads onto the fish for eyes.

CATCH OF THE DAY

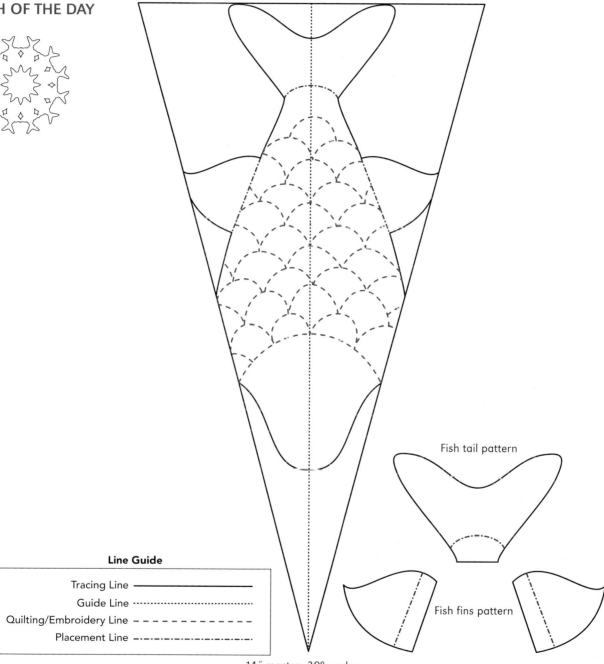

Fish tail pattern

Fish fins pattern

Line Guide

Tracing Line	———————
Guide Line	··················
Quilting/Embroidery Line	– – – – – – –
Placement Line	–·–·–·–·–·–

14″ master—30° wedge

FISH NET

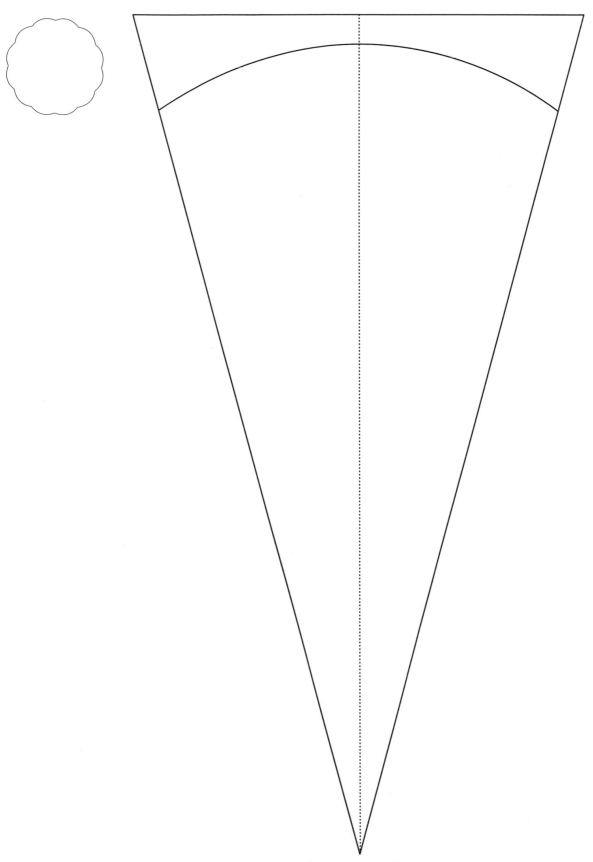

18″ master—30° wedge

Bridal Tea

72″ × 72″, 2006, Kathy K. Wylie

Bridal Tea is a story of women and heritage and tradition. My grandmother collected beautiful china teacups, as did my mother, my aunt, and my husband's grandmother. Some of these treasures have made their way to my own collection.

The teacups were brought out for special occasions, for those times when women gather— for bridal showers and trousseau teas. Fancy sandwiches and dainty squares would be served on tiered serving plates, and the tea and coffee poured from the polished silver tea service.

Didn't we also pretend these things as little girls with our first toy tea sets?

Perhaps tea parties are becoming a thing of the past. But for me, they are a part of the women of my past, my heritage and maternal tradition.

Fabric Requirements

Based on 40″ fabric width.

DESCRIPTION	EXAMPLE	YARDS	METERS
Background fabric	Yellow	$3\frac{1}{8}$	2.90
SEWFLAKES FABRIC			
My Cup of Tea	Dark purple*	$3\frac{1}{4}$	3.00
Dresden Plate centers			
Accent border strip			
Binding			
DRESDEN PLATE FABRIC			
Fabric 1	Yellow/green print	$\frac{3}{8}$	0.35
Fabric 2	Medium violet	$\frac{3}{8}$	0.35
Fabric 3	Violet /yellow floral	$\frac{3}{8}$	0.35
Fabric 4	Dark violet	$\frac{3}{8}$	0.35
OUTER BORDER	Teacups print	$2\frac{1}{3}$	2.00

*There are 3 dark purple fabrics used in the sample. Total combined yardage listed.

Cutting Instructions

Unless otherwise noted, strips are cut across the width of the fabric.

NUMBER OF STRIPS	WIDTH	FIRST CUT QUANTITY	FIRST CUT SIZE	SECOND CUT
BACKGROUND FABRIC (SEE CUTTING DIAGRAM)				
From 60″ length of fabric:				
Border 1			4	$4\frac{1}{2}″ \times 60″$
Block			3	$16\frac{1}{2}″ \times 16\frac{1}{2}″$
From remaining fabric:				
Block			6	$16\frac{1}{2}″ \times 16\frac{1}{2}″$
SEWFLAKES FABRIC—MY CUP OF TEA				
Block	5	$16\frac{1}{2}″$	9	$16\frac{1}{2}″ \times 16\frac{1}{2}″$
Accent strip	8	1″		
Binding	8	$2\frac{1}{2}″$		
DRESDEN PLATE FABRICS (CUT FROM EACH OF 4 FABRICS)				
Patch A	5	$2\frac{1}{4}″$	36	$2\frac{1}{4}″ \times 4\frac{1}{2}″$
OUTER BORDER (CUT FROM LENGTH OF FABRIC)				
Border 2	4	$8\frac{1}{2}″$		

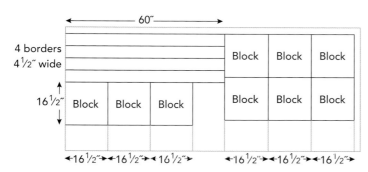

Background fabric cutting diagram

Other Supplies

Template material (freezer paper, fusible web, or water-soluble stabilizer):

Nine $16\frac{1}{2}″ \times 16\frac{1}{2}″$ pieces for My Cup of Tea sewflakes

Nine $2\frac{3}{4}″ \times 2\frac{3}{4}″$ pieces for Dresden Plate centers

Nine $9\frac{1}{2}″ \times 9\frac{1}{2}″$ pieces for Dresden Plates (optional)

Template plastic

Block Assembly

DRESDEN PLATE BLOCKS

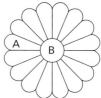

1. Using the patterns on page 55, cut plastic templates of Patch A and Patch B.

2. Trace the template of Patch A onto the wrong sides of $2\frac{1}{4}″ \times 4\frac{1}{2}″$ Dresden Plate fabrics. Cut the fabric on the traced line. Trace and cut 144 of Patch A (36 each from 4 different fabrics).

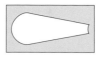

3. Sew a Fabric 1 Patch A to a Fabric 2 Patch A along the straight edge. Press. Make 36. Sew a Fabric 3 Patch A to a Fabric 4 Patch A along the straight edge. Press. Make 36.

Make 36.   Make 36.

4. Sew a Fabric 1/Fabric 2 pair to a Fabric 3/Fabric 4 pair. Press. Make 36.

Make 36.

5. Sew 2 of these units together to form half a Dresden Plate. Press. Make 18.

Make 18.

6. Sew 2 halves together to complete the Dresden Plate. Press. Make 9.

Make 9.

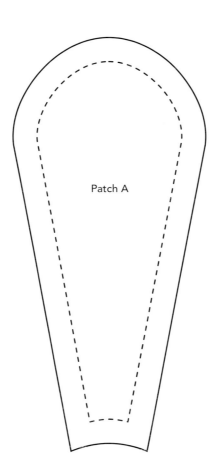

Patch A

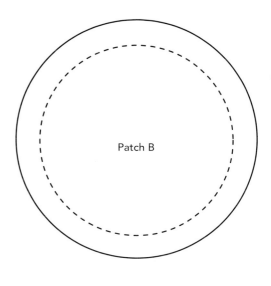

Patch B

SEWFLAKE BLOCKS

My Cup of Tea block

1. Using the *Bridal Tea* patterns on page 57, transfer each sewflake from the master wedge to a 16½˝ × 16½˝ square of the template material of your choice (see Preparing a Sewflake Pattern, pages 15–18). Keep the following in mind:

a. The My Cup of Tea sewflake repeats the master wedge 4 times.

b. My Cup of Tea is nonsymmetrical; be sure to use a reverse master wedge if you will be transferring the sewflake to the wrong side of the fabric.

c. My Cup of Tea is also an outer image. This sewflake will be appliquéd to the outside edges of the block.

 Note

See the tip on page 16 if the template material is not wide enough for the designs.

2. Transfer the sewflake design to a 16½˝ × 16½˝ square of sewflake fabric, according to your chosen appliqué method. I used needle-turn hand appliqué for this quilt. There will be a ¼˝-wide seam allowance around the outside edges.

3. Appliqué the sewflake to a 16½˝ × 16½˝ square of background fabric.

Appliqué Dresden Plate Blocks

1. Center a Dresden Plate onto a My Cup of Tea appliquéd block. Appliqué in place.

2. Trace the template of Patch B onto a scrap of sewflake fabric. Cut the fabric on the traced line.

3. Appliqué Patch B in the center of the Dresden Plate.

Bridal Tea assembly diagram

Quilt Assembly

1. Consulting the assembly diagram, sew 3 blocks together to form a row. Press. Make 3 rows of 3 blocks each.

2. Sew the rows together. Press.

3. Measure the length and width of the quilt through the center. Mark the center on the top and bottom Border 1 strips. Measuring from the center out, mark half of the width measurement. Repeat for the other end. Align the marks and sew the borders onto the quilt, starting and stopping the seam $1/4''$ from the edges. Pin the side Border 1 strips to the quilt, matching the center and the quilt length measurement. Sew the borders onto the quilt, starting and stopping the seam $1/4''$ from the edges. Miter the corner seams.

4. Sew 2 accent strips together end-to-end. Make 4. Fold in half, wrong sides together, to form $1/2''$-wide strips. Press. Cut the strips to the same length and width measurements used in Step 3. With raw edges together and the folded edge in toward the center, sew an accent strip onto each edge of Border 1. The accent strip stays in this position to form a dimensional border.

5. Repeat Step 3 to apply Border 2 strips to the quilt. Press.

6. Arrange backing, batting and quilt top together. Hand or machine quilt, as desired. Attach the binding.

Bridal Tea
SEWFLAKE PATTERNS

MY CUP OF TEA

Line Guide
Tracing Line
Registration Line
Seam Line
Add ¼″ to seam
Add ¼″ to seam
16″ master—90° wedge

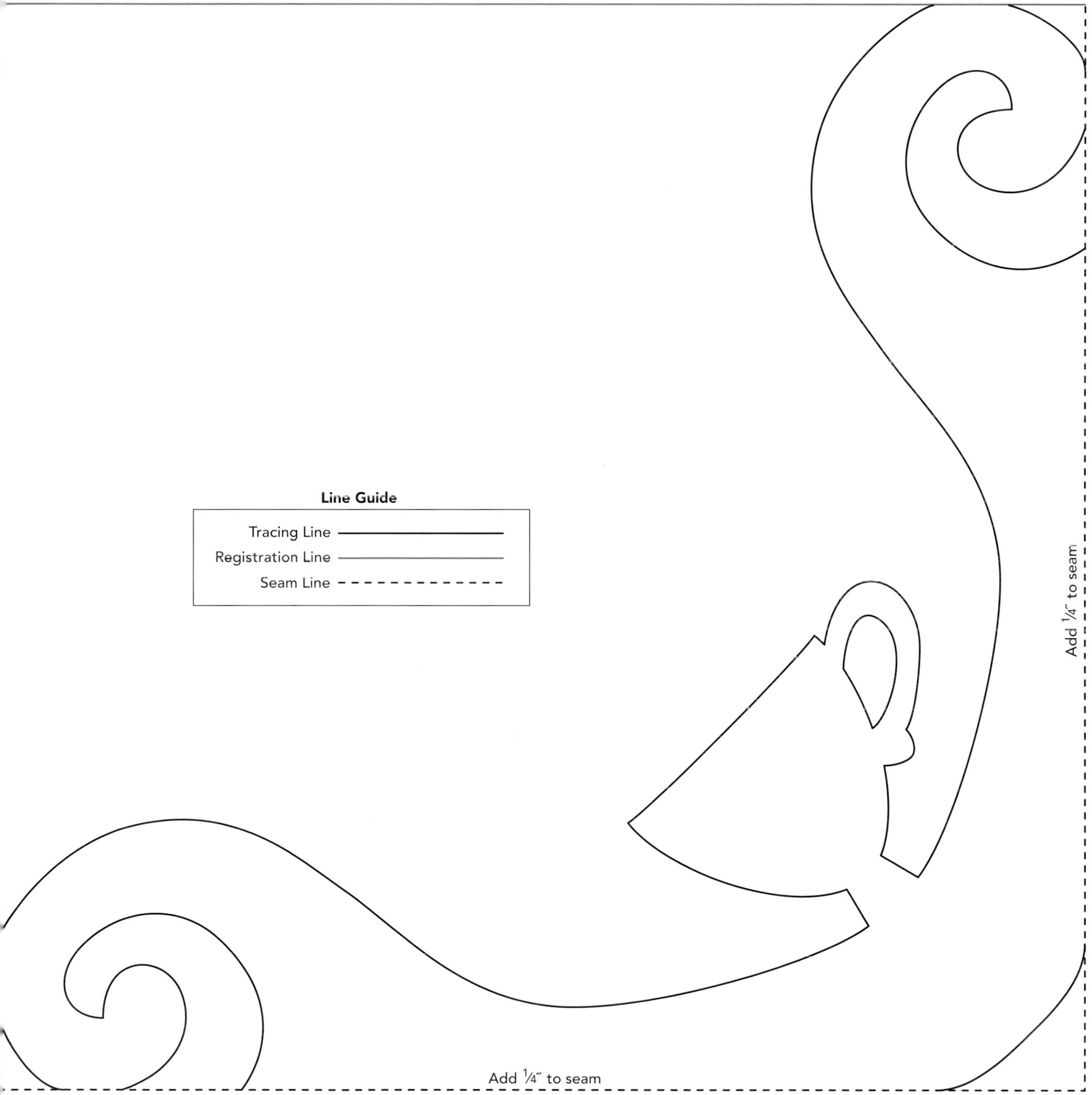

King of Hearts

48″ × 48″, 2007, Kathy K. Wylie

King of Hearts is based on a deck of cards. The four suits—diamonds, clubs, spades, and hearts—surround a Card Trick block. The quilt also speaks about the things we value in life.

Money and
possessions

Pleasing people

Those we love

Our work

Who is King of your heart?

Fabric Requirements

Based on 40″ fabric width.

DESCRIPTION	EXAMPLE	YARDS	METERS
Black background fabric	Black*	1⅝	1.50
Red background fabric	Red*	1⅛	1.10
Sewflakes fabric	White	1	0.90
Card fabric	Red/black/white print	⅞	0.80

*There are 2 black fabrics and 2 red fabrics used in the sample.
Total combined yardage listed.

Cutting Instructions

Unless otherwise noted, strips are cut across the width of the fabric.

NUMBER OF STRIPS	WIDTH	FIRST CUT QUANTITY	FIRST CUT SIZE	SECOND CUT
BLACK BACKGROUND FABRIC				
Background 1	12½″	2	12½″ × 12½″	
		2	12½″ × 6½″	
1	6½″	2	6½″ × 12½″	
Patch C 1	5¼″	1	5¼″ × 5¼″	In quarters diagonally
Patch A		3	4⅞″ × 4⅞″	In half diagonally
Patch B		2	2⅞″ × 2⅞″	In half diagonally
Patch G		2	3⅞″ × 3⅞″	In half diagonally
Patch F 3	4¼″	26	4¼″ × 4¼″	In quarters diagonally
Binding 6	2½″			
RED BACKGROUND FABRIC				
Background 1	12½″	2	12½″ × 12½″	
		2	12½″ × 6½″	
1	6½″	2	6½″ × 12½″	
Patch A 1	4⅞″	1	4⅞″ × 4⅞″	In half diagonally
Patch B		2	2⅞″ × 2⅞″	In half diagonally
Patch G		2	3⅞″ × 3⅞″	In half diagonally
Patch E 3	2⅝″	40	2⅝″ × 2⅝″	
Patch F 1	4¼″	6	4¼″ × 4¼″	In quarters diagonally
SEWFLAKES FABRIC				
Sewflakes 2	14″	4	14″ × 14″	
Accent strips 4	1″	2	1″ × 36½″	
		2	1″ × 35½″	
CARD FABRIC				
Patch C 1	5¼″	1	5¼″ × 5¼″	In quarters diagonally
Patch A		2	4⅞″ × 4⅞″	In half diagonally
Patch D 4	4¾″	28	4¾″ × 4¾″	

Other Supplies

Template material (freezer paper, fusible web, or water-soluble stabilizer):

Four 14″ × 14″ pieces for sewflakes

Machine embroidery thread (optional, for satin stitching sewflakes)

Block Assembly

CARD TRICK BLOCK

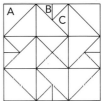

Unit 1

1. Sew a red Patch B to a black Patch B. Press. Make 2 with red on the left and 2 with black on the left.

Make 2 of each.

2. Sew a black Patch C to the triangle pairs with red on the left. Press. Make 2.

Make 2.

3. Sew a print Patch C to the triangle pairs with black on the left. Press. Make 2.

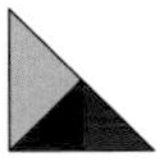

Make 2.

4. Sew a print Patch A to a black/red/black triangle unit. Press. Make 2. Sew a black Patch A to a print/black/red triangle unit. Press. Make 2. Unit 1 should measure $4^{1}/_{2}'' \times 4^{1}/_{2}''$.

Make 2 of each.

Unit 2

Sew a black Patch A to a red Patch A. Press. Make 2. Sew a black Patch A to a print Patch A. Press. Make 2. Unit 2 should measure $4^{1}/_{2}'' \times 4^{1}/_{2}''$.

Make 2 of each.

Unit 3

1. Sew a black Patch C to a print Patch C. Press. Make 2. Sew the triangles together. Press. Unit 3 should measure $4^{1}/_{2}'' \times 4^{1}/_{2}''$.

Make 2.   Make 1.

2. Referring to the diagram below, sew the blocks together as shown. Press. The Card Trick block should measure $12^{1}/_{2}'' \times 12^{1}/_{2}''$.

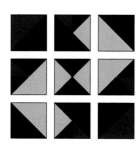

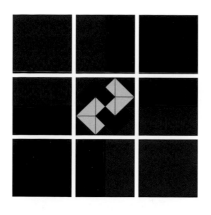

BACKGROUND ASSEMBLY

1. Sew black and red $12^{1}/_{2}'' \times 6^{1}/_{2}''$ rectangles together. Press. Make 4.

2. Arrange and sew background blocks and Card Trick block together as shown. Press. The background should measure $36^{1}/_{2}'' \times 36^{1}/_{2}''$.

SEWFLAKE BLOCKS

Diamonds Are Forever block

Join the Club block

Call a Spade a Spade block

All My Heart block

1. Using the *King of Hearts* patterns on pages 62–63, transfer each sewflake from the master wedge to a $14'' \times 14''$ square of the template material of your choice (see Preparing a Sewflake Pattern, pages 15–18). Keep the following in mind:

    a. The *King of Hearts* sewflakes repeat the master wedge 12 times and are symmetrical designs.

    b. After each design is transferred, add the single motif to the center of the sewflake.

 See the tip on page 16 if the template material is not wide enough for the design.

2. Prepare the sewflake fabric according to the appliqué method of your choice. I used cutwork appliqué for this quilt.

3. Using a removable marker that is visible on the background fabrics, draw lines 9″ out from the center. The sewflakes will be centered on these lines.

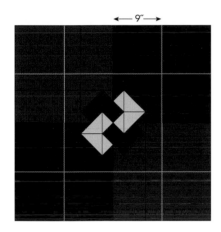

4. Appliqué All My Heart and Diamonds Are Forever onto the red background, centered on the marked lines. Appliqué Join the Club and Call a Spade a Spade onto the black background, centered on the marked lines. Make sure that each single motif in the center of the sewflake is oriented in the same direction.

Quilt Assembly

1. Trim the quilt top to $35^1/2″ \times 35^1/2″$ by measuring $17^3/4″$ from the center.

2. Sew two $1″ \times 35^1/2″$ accent strips to the sides of the quilt top. Press. Sew two $1″ \times 36^1/2″$ accent strips to the top and the bottom. Press. The quilt top should again measure $36^1/2″ \times 36^1/2″$.

PIECED BORDER

Make 40.

1. Sew a black Patch F to 2 sides of a red Patch E as shown. Press. Make 40.

Make 12 of each.

2. Sew a black Patch F to a red Patch F. Make 12 with black on the left and 12 with red on the left. Press.

3. Using these triangle units from Steps 1 and 2 and the print D Patches, assemble 4 borders according to the diagram below.

Make 4.

CORNER BORDER BLOCKS

1. Sew a red Patch G to one side of a print Patch D, and a black Patch G to the other side, as shown. Press.

Make 4.

2. Sew the remaining red/black Patch F triangles from the Pieced Border, Step 2, to the remaining sides of a unit from Step 1, lining up the colors with the G Patches as shown. Press. Make 4.

3. Referring to the assembly diagram and diagram in Step 4 below, sew a pieced border onto the top and bottom of the quilt. Press.

4. Sew a corner block onto both ends of the remaining 2 pieced borders. Press.

King of Hearts assembly diagram

5. Referring to the assembly diagram, sew the borders from Step 4 to the sides of the quilt. Press. The quilt top should measure $48^1/2″ \times 48^1/2″$.

6. Arrange backing, batting and quilt top together. Hand or machine quilt, as desired. Attach the binding.

King of Hearts
SEWFLAKE PATTERNS

DIAMONDS ARE FOREVER

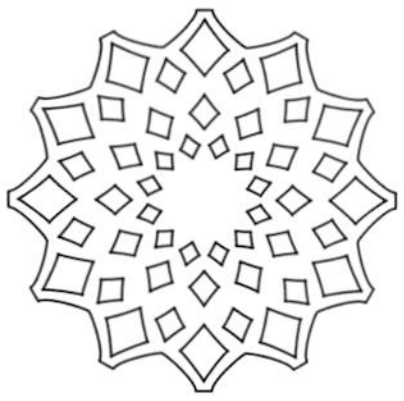

Line Guide

Tracing Line ———————
Guide Line ·····················

14″ master—30° wedge

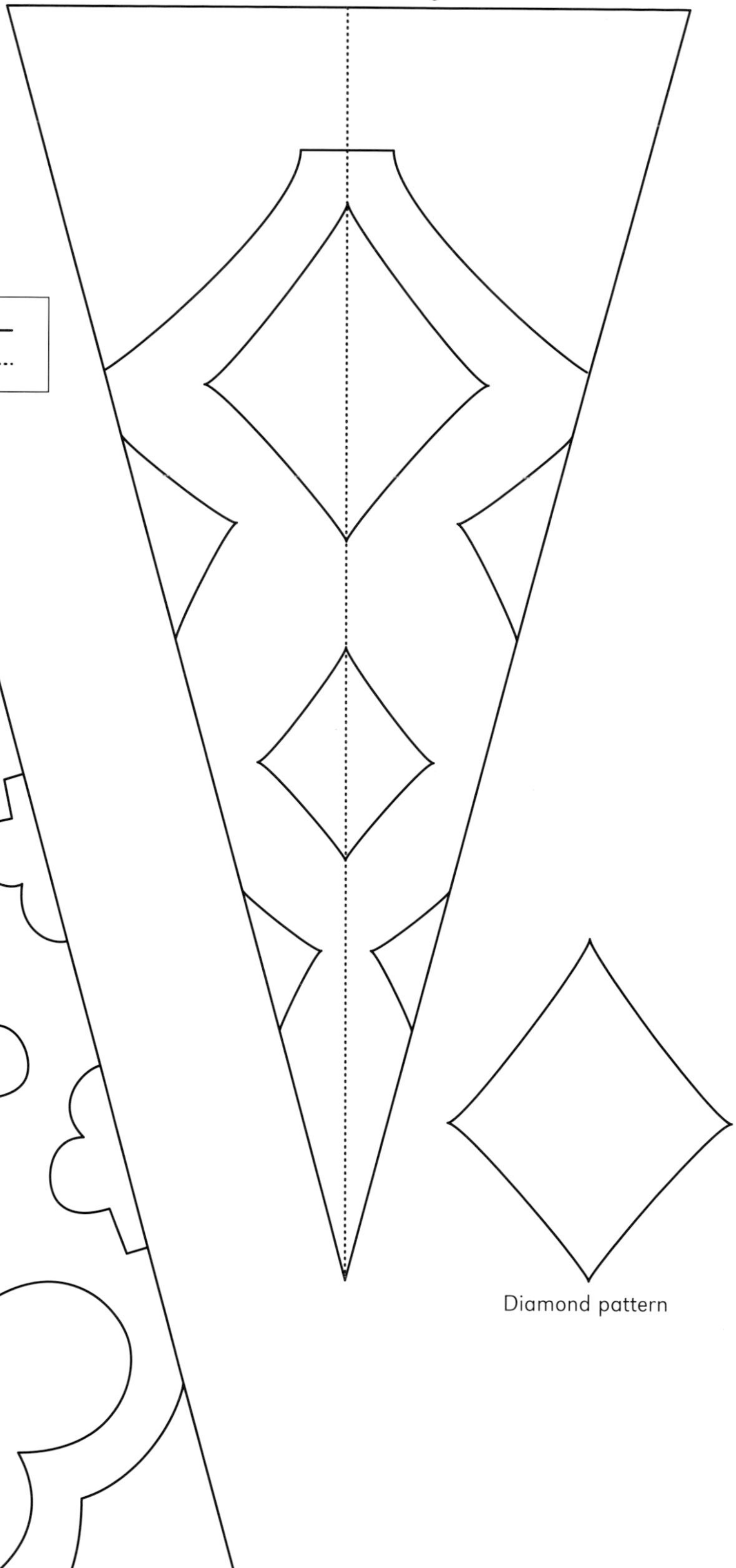

Diamond pattern

Club pattern

JOIN THE CLUB

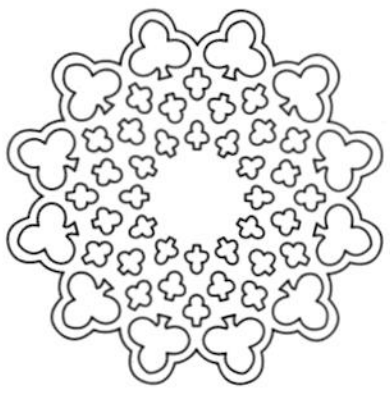

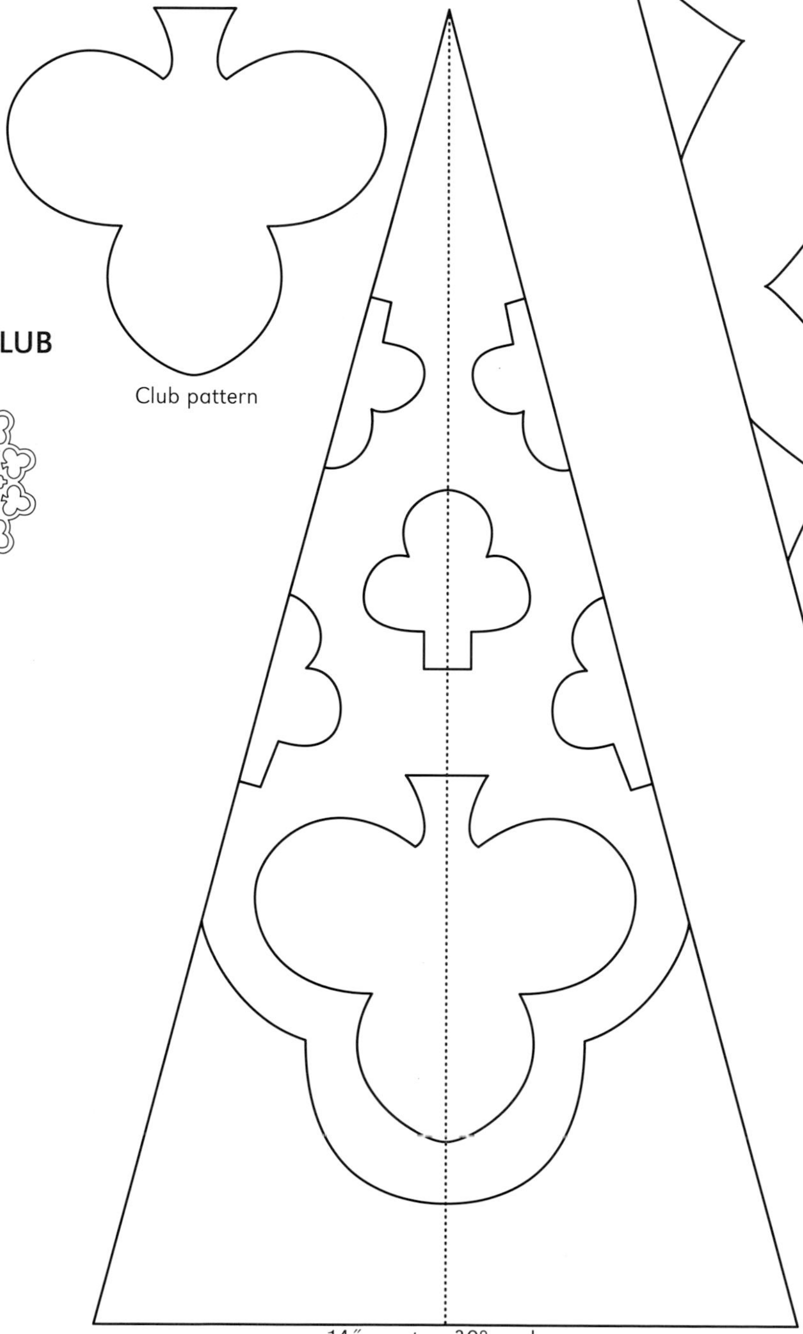

14″ master—30° wedge

CALL A SPADE A SPADE

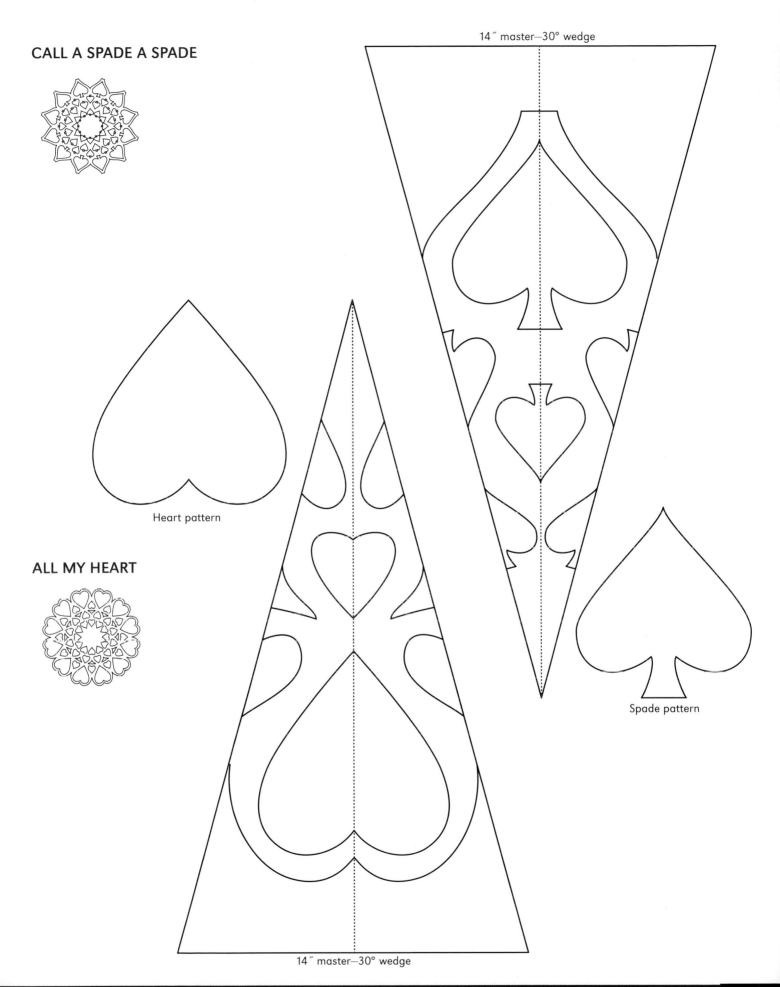

14″ master—30° wedge

Heart pattern

ALL MY HEART

Spade pattern

14″ master—30° wedge

Resources

For a list of other fine books from C&T Publishing, ask for a free catalog:

C&T PUBLISHING, INC.
P.O. Box 1456
Lafayette, CA 94549
(800) 284-1114
Email: ctinfo@ctpub.com
Website: www.ctpub.com
C&T Publishing's professional photography services are now available to the public. Visit us at
www.ctmediaservices.com.

For quilting supplies:

COTTON PATCH
1025 Brown Ave.
Lafayette, CA 94549
(800) 835-4418 or
(925) 283-7883
Email: CottonPa@aol.com
Website: www.quiltusa.com
Note: Fabrics used in the quilts shown may not be currently available, as fabric manufacturers keep most fabrics in print for only a short time.

EQ5 and Blockbase

THE ELECTRIC QUILT COMPANY
419 Gould Street, Suite 2
Bowling Green, OH 43402-3047
www.electricquilt.com

Pacific Rim Quilt Company

NANCY LEE CHONG &
JANICE LEE BAEHR
P.O. Box 932
Snohomish, WA 98291-0932
www.prqc.com
Pattern for *"Midnight on the Oasis"* is available as *"Orchid Oasis."*

Books

Encyclopedia of Pieced Quilt Patterns by Barbara Brackman, American Quilter's Society, 1993

A Treasury of Quilting Designs by Linda Goodmon Emery, American Quilter's Society, 1990

The Best of Baltimore Beauties, Books 1 and 2, by Elly Sienkiewicz, C&T Publishing, 2000 and 2002

About the Author

Kathy K. Wylie

Photo by Alexander Robertson Photography

Kathy was introduced to needle arts at a very young age. Throughout her childhood, she spent summers at the family cottage learning to knit with her grandmother and practicing crochet and needlepoint embroidery with her aunt. Her mother taught her to sew and was, for the rest of the year, her willing accomplice and frequent partner in pattern searches, fabric shopping expeditions, and garment fittings. But when the time came to choose an occupation, it didn't occur to Kathy to study the arts. Considering her crafts a hobby, she majored in Information Systems and graduated from McGill University in 1984 with a Bachelor of Commerce degree. This led to a career in the computer industry selling banking systems.

After opting to leave her job to stay home and raise her family, Kathy took her first quilting class in the spring of 1994. It was love at first sight—quilting was the perfect combination of everything she enjoyed. Kathy's passion for quilting has only continued to grow. She teaches quilting classes at guilds, quilting conferences, and quilt shops. Her award-winning original designs have been displayed in quilt exhibitions worldwide, and her warm and enthusiastic quilting presentations have inspired many an audience.

Kathy is interested in a broad spectrum of quilting techniques, but her style would best be described as "contemporary traditional." She became fascinated with papercut appliqué because of its possibilities for incorporating subtle imagery into her quilts. As Kathy has developed as an artist, her work has taken on a distinct focus. Her quilts convey messages of faith and hope and are a reflection of her relationship with God.

Kathy is Canadian and lives with her husband and two sons in the town of Whitby, just east of Toronto, Ontario. She still spends summers at the cottage, only now she quilts!

Visit Kathy on the web at www.kathykwylie.com.